D0461144

COLOR

Better Homes and Gardens®

SOLUTIONS

Better Homes and Gardens® Books
Des Moines, Iowa

Better Homes and Gardens® Books
An imprint of Meredith® Books

Better Homes and Gardens® Color Solutions
Editor: Vicki L. Ingham
Senior Associate Art Director: Ken Carlson
Copy Chief: Terri Fredrickson
Copy and Production Editor: Victoria Forlini
Editorial Operations Manager: Karen Schirm
Managers, Book Production: Pam Kvitne, Marjorie J. Schenkelberg
Contributing Copy Editor: Jane Woychick
Contributing Proofreaders: Maria Duryee, Nancy Ruhling, Susan Sanfrey
Contributing Photographers: Cheryl Dalton, Peter Krumhardt
Indexer: Barbara L. Klein
Electronic Production Coordinator: Paula Forest
Editorial and Design Assistants: Kaye Chabot, Mary Lee Gavin

Meredith® Books
Editor in Chief: James D. Blume
Design Director: Matt Strelecki
Managing Editor: Gregory H. Kayko
Executive Editor, Home Decorating and Design: Denise L. Caringer

Director, Sales, Special Markets: Rita McMullen
Director, Sales, Premiums: Michael A. Peterson
Director, Sales, Retail: Tom Wierzbicki
Director, Book Marketing: Brad Elmitt
Director, Operations: George A. Susral
Director, Production: Douglas M. Johnston

Vice President and General Manager: Douglas J. Guendel

Better Homes and Gardens® Magazine
Editor in Chief: Karol DeWulf Nickell
Executive Building Editor: Joan McCloskey
Executive Interior Design Editor: Sandra S. Soria

Meredith Publishing Group
President, Publishing Group: Stephen M. Lacy
Vice President-Publishing Director: Bob Mate

Meredith Corporation
Chairman and Chief Executive Officer: William T. Kerr

Chairman of the Executive Committee: E. T. Meredith III

Copyright © 2002 by Meredith Corporation, Des Moines, Iowa. First Edition.
All rights reserved. Printed in the United States of America.
Library of Congress Control Number: 2001135116
ISBN: 0-696-21240-4

All of us at Better Homes and Gardens® Books are dedicated to providing you with information and ideas to enhance your home. We welcome your comments and suggestions. Write to us at: Better Homes and Gardens Books, Home Decorating and Design Editorial Department, 1716 Locust St., Des Moines, IA 50309-3023.

If you would like to purchase any of our home decorating and design, cooking, crafts, gardening, or home improvement books, check wherever quality books are sold. Or visit us at: bhgbooks.com

Cover Photograph: Philip Clayton Thompson

As an artist, I love color and I use it in my paintings to capture the quality of light at various times of day. I'm drawn to strong colors—one of my favorite combinations is deep blue-purple and warm cadmium yellow. Working on canvas, however, is different from painting a room. On my first venture into bold colors for my home, I made the classic mistake of thinking the blue on the little paint chip would yield the lovely periwinkle I'd seen at a designer showhouse. It turned out to be an intense laser blue that was awful. That experience taught me that painting may be the easiest way to change your rooms, but it's still an investment of time and money—and who has either to waste?

From reading the decorating discussions on the *Better Homes and Gardens*® website, I know that making that investment is one of the biggest challenges people wrestle with. Those discussion groups inspired this book: I chose 10 of the most frequently asked questions and then worked with homeowners and interior designers around the country to find

INTRODUCTION

examples of workable options. Note the word "options"—there's no one answer to any of the questions about where and how to use color, because color is intensely personal. By studying a variety of solutions to the same color question, you'll be able to identify the one that creates the look and feeling you want in your home.

In the Resources section (pages 162–165), you'll find information about paints and fabrics, but please remember that the color you see on the printed page may look nothing like the paint in the can or the fabric on the bolt. The appearance of a color alters as the type and intensity of light in which you see it changes. When you add in the effects of film, ink, and the printing process, it's nearly impossible to reproduce accurately in a book the color the homeowner sees on the walls, ceiling, and furniture. If you fall in love with a color on the printed page, take the book to a paint store and look for paint chips that resemble the color in the photo. Then test the paint on poster board to see how you like it. Finding the right colors for your home may take some experimenting, but it's worth the effort—wonderful color makes the heart sing.

Vicki Ingham

Vicki Ingham
Editor, *Color Solutions*

CONTENTS

Linking rooms with color may not seem very important if your rooms can be separated from each other by closing doors. If you can see from one room into another, however, the color relationships between those rooms affect whether your living space feels smoothly harmonious or jarringly chopped up. Using unrelated colors in adjoining rooms can make the house feel like a disjointed series of spaces, while colors that relate to each other draw the eye from one room to the next and create a pleasing flow. In a house with an open floor plan or one in which rooms connect through wide openings, it's even more important to choose colors that relate to each other in a pleasing way. In this situation, the challenge is to give each space its own identity according to its function and still achieve a feeling of unity. On the

QUESTION 1

HOW DO I CONNECT ROOMS WITH COLOR?

pages that follow, you'll find examples of options for knitting spaces together with color. If you love lots of color, you can still achieve flow by choosing one hue to be a unifying thread that runs from room to room. Usually this unifying element is the woodwork—baseboards, door and window frames, and molding at the ceiling. The connection can be more subtle, too, such as a recurring color in the fabrics, accessories, and furniture in each room. You also can achieve a feeling of continuity by limiting your palette to two or three colors that you use in different amounts and applications throughout the house. Each color can be used in different values and intensities to produce a wide range of effects.

One way to create a feeling of flow when each room is a different color is to repeat one hue in every room. Furniture, accessories, and trim can carry the thread of color through the house.

OPTION 1 USE A THREAD OF COLOR.

Give each room its own color personality while ensuring a cohesive feeling by using a single hue as a theme that runs throughout. In this 19th-century Charleston, South Carolina, house, the black marble mantels in the living and dining rooms provided the cue for the thread of black that links all rooms in the house. In the two formal rooms and the entry, designer Amelia T. Handegan had a decorative painter marbleize the baseboards and apply a black and white diamond pattern to the entry floor. For the walls in these areas,

Handegan chose warm colors that would coordinate with each other yet give each space a different feeling.

The living room embraces its occupants with a warm melon color inspired by the drapery fabric; the golden yellow in the dining room springs from antique cornices found for the windows. To ease the transition between these two colors, Handegan chose a paler yellow for the entry walls. The black and gilt cornices in the dining room then inspired the search for the black furnishings and upholstery fabrics that recur in every room. In the living room, a 19th-century

Painting the walls to match the drapery fabric creates an envelope of color in the room. The fabric blends with the background yet adds softness and dimension to the walls. Check with your local paint dealer about custom-mixing paints to match a solid-color fabric.

Q. HOW DO I CONNECT ROOMS WITH COLOR?

English chinoiserie secretary and French ebonized chairs, and antique tables supply the note of black and serve as background color. They're not the first things you notice when you walk in, but they quietly anchor the room. In the dining room, black is more prominent, appearing in the chair fabric and major furnishings. The dark furnishings don't become oppressive, however, because the walls capture the impression of sunshine and the carpet and ceiling reflect light as well.

Door and window frames are painted a creamy white to make the wall colors look crisp and fresh. The contrast with the baseboard calls more attention to the baseboard, so this approach works best if the baseboard is substantial in proportion to the height of the wall.

TOP: Black and gold antique cornices inspired the dining room color scheme. The designer had the wall color custom-mixed to match the drapery fabric. ABOVE: Sisal carpet covers the floor with a light-reflecting neutral color, enhancing the sense of space. An antique rug lies over the sisal to provide a visual anchor for the dining table. Double-stick carpet pad under the rug prevents "carpet creep." Black and white check fabric freshens the early-20th-century French cane-back chairs. OPPOSITE: Bright yellow and black was a favorite color combination in the Napoleonic era. The high-contrast pairing could seem harsh, but here it is softened by the worn patina on the chairs and antique dining table. By candlelight or firelight, the room becomes a golden cocoon.

PLAY IT AGAIN ... AND AGAIN ... AND AGAIN Repetition is the key to creating unity in a painting, a song, or a series of rooms. The repeating note—in this house, the color black—can appear in upholstery, pillows, and accessories, as well as in the architecture. Black marbleized baseboards and stair risers link the living room, dining room, and entry hall. The den, *below*, is trimmed entirely in creamy white, but the black theme continues in the upholstery, coffee table, lampshade, and pillows. In any color scheme, a touch of black adds depth; using it as the common thread creates a rich, understated elegance, whether you combine it with bright, bold colors or muted neutrals.

In the den, Handegan chose a light gray for the walls and painted the baseboards the same creamy white as the window frames and crown molding for a clean, open look. Here and in the study (see pages 14–15) the furniture and accessories carry the unifying thread of color: black leather on the French armchair, black and white ticking on the love seat, a 1930s chinoiserie table, and a black lampshade. Gleaming hardwood floors and rich accents of brown, ocher, and red warm the black.

Using furnishings and accessories to create color flow is like having a color-coordinated wardrobe—you can mix and match, creating new looks whenever you want a change. The French armchair in the den would be just as at home in the living room, for example, or the ticking-covered love seat in the den could move upstairs to the office. This kind of flexibility is most easily achieved with neutrals because they can work in a variety of settings. The black-upholstered and ebonized-wood pieces in this home, for example, look handsome against yellow and melon walls as well as against gray and brown; they also would be dramatic in rooms painted red or bright yellow-green.

If you're shopping for end tables, consider antique bamboo. The mottled black and brown coloration fits quietly into any color scheme, and the slender lines suit contemporary small spaces as well as the grander proportions of older homes.

ABOVE: In the study, black baseboards, the fireplace surround, and armchairs covered in suede continue the thread of color. **OPPOSITE:** A wax finish on the faux-grained mantel brings out mustard gold tones that contrast subtly with the chocolate-taupe walls and draw attention to the room's focal point.

In the study, black baseboards and chairs covered in black suede bring the color theme upstairs. The window frames and bookcases are painted to match the suede-covered walls. Blending walls and woodwork in this way minimizes architectural elements that would otherwise break up the walls—a good technique for enlarging the sense of space in a small room. When you limit the distractions of contrasting color and shape, you also effectively invoke a serene atmosphere. Accents, like the red in the pillow and area rug, supply a jolt of bright color that enlivens the monochromatic color scheme.

OPTION 2 SET UP A DIALOGUE.

New houses often feature kitchens and great-rooms that connect phys-ically and visually, separated only by a partial wall or counter. To paint each area a different color, use the partial wall or peninsula as the dividing line. Unify the two areas by using the same trim color through-out, and reinforce that connection by bringing touches of each area's color into the other. For a smooth transi-tion, choose two col-ors that are closely related and similar in value. Here, a soft periwinkle blue colors the gar-den room, and an equally gentle celery green brightens the kitchen. A close shade of the green upholsters two armchairs in the garden room; the periwinkle blue enters the kitchen in the floor tile and chair seats. The cobalt blue window seat punctuates the garden room with an exclamation mark of vivid color. (This is a good way to introduce a bold color that you love but can't immerse yourself in.) If you like the drama and energy of higher contrast, you could select colors from opposite sides of the color wheel, such as violet and yellow or salmon and sage green.

OPTION 3 UNIFY WITH WHITE TRIM.

Painting all of the trim throughout the house the same color of white is a no-fail way to create a sense of flow from room to room. There are many shades of white, so select your wall colors first, then choose a white that works with all of them. In the house shown *below* and on the following pages, a sour-cream white contrasts crisply with the bold colors and harmonizes with the softer ones.

In developing the color scheme for this house, interior designer Roberta Ketchin selected vibrant colors that would create an elegant yet relaxed mood. From the entry, visitors can see both the dining room and the living room as well as the hall on the second floor. A wallpaper with a stucco finish links the entry, living room, stairwell, and upstairs hall, emphasizing this area's openness and the way the spaces flow into one another. A color-wash effect on the wallpaper

OPPOSITE: Ceramic tile makes a practical, durable flooring for a kitchen that accommodates a large family. The floor inspired the choice of celery green for the walls and ceiling. Fabrics in a mix of florals and prints pull the green of the kitchen into the garden room. BELOW: In an open floor plan, unify a multicolor scheme by using a single color for the trim. If you have an entry, stair, and living room that run together without interruption, use the same wall color throughout to enlarge the sense of space.

Q. HOW DO I CONNECT ROOMS WITH COLOR?

layers several tones of cream, café au lait, and a touch of cabernet, giving the walls a subtle depth. In the dining room, which is framed by a cased opening and columns, Ketchin custom-mixed a red that matches the color of a camellia in her garden.

The white trim ensures that these spaces will look connected, and Ketchin reinforces the effect with subliminal cues or markers to make people feel anchored as they move through the house. In this house, says the designer, the color scheme was devised to give each room a different feeling while relating each to the others by means of repeated recognizable color elements. These elements help link one room to the next. In the living room, the sofa and throw pillows echo the color of the dining room walls. In the dining room, chair cushions reiterate the note of yellow-green that appears in the plaid upholstery on a living room chair.

In the kitchen, the bleached, wormy-maple cabinets might have suggested a South-of-France or Italian country look, if the walls were yellow or terra-cotta. Instead, Ketchin chose a green the color of grass or palmetto. The cool color gives the room depth and complements the wood of the cabinetry. "It's a big room," she says, "like a big box. The cool color on the walls pushes them back. To get the warmth I wanted, I used a vibrant, warm yellow on the ceiling. So you have a tension between the warm ceiling and cool walls that makes the room inviting and offsets all the cabinetry."

OPPOSITE: In the entry, Ketchin created a focal point with a small mahogany chest, a painted Oriental chair, and an area rug. Flowers have a role to play too. Red roses or a magenta orchid are always displayed on the chest for a welcoming splash of color. CENTER: White trim brightens intense wall colors. BELOW: From the entry, visitors see the dining room and a sliver of the kitchen, which is a bright green. White woodwork connects the two.

Use accessories to accent a color scheme. A tomato red vase trimmed with green punches up the kitchen's green and yellow palette. OPPOSITE: White trim leads the eye from the green kitchen into the terracotta family room. Fabrics and accessories finish the job of tying the two spaces together. Green brings a cooler feeling to spaces because it lies on the cool side of the color wheel and because it calls to mind shady trees and mossy glades. Use it to lower the perceived temperature in a sun-filled room that faces south.

Q. HOW DO I CONNECT ROOMS WITH COLOR?

OPTION 4 CHOOSE A LIMITED PALETTE.

Open floor plans, whether in a suburban home, a condominium, or an apartment, allow architects to maximize the feeling of space without increasing square footage. That doesn't mean you have to paint all of the connecting spaces one color, however. One way to give each area its own personality and still achieve a unified look is to choose two or three colors that work well together and use them in varying amounts from room to room. In this Houston condominium, the homeowner selected her favorite colors—a patriotic palette of red, white, and blue—to decorate the entry, living and dining areas, and kitchen. Each of these areas can be seen from the others, so limiting the palette guarantees that each view will be pleasing.

Homeowner Anne Kinder is an artist who loves strong color. "All my life I've loved red and white check," she says. "I love red. It makes me feel happy." That's why she chose the color for her large entry hall and kitchen. Getting just the right red required several trips to the paint store and mixing until she got the right shade, neither too orange nor too blue. The red entry leads to an equally intense blue living-dining room. "The blue had to be bright enough to balance the red," Anne notes.

WHAT'S UNDERFOOT If you paint adjoining rooms in strongly contrasting colors, connect them by using area rugs that include both colors. The red and powder blue Oriental rug in Anne Kinder's living area anchors her scheme by repeating the wall colors on the floor. The wall and rug hues don't have to match exactly; one can be slightly darker or lighter than the other, and the eye will still perceive them as closely related.

PLAYING WITH STRIPES AND CHECKS In the long, narrow kitchen, Anne combined the red with white in stripes and checks (see pages 24–25). "We were looking for interest," explains architect Tony Tamborello. "All red within the narrow space would be too much." Stripes on the end wall where the breakfast table stands provide a focal point that helps bring the wall forward, visually shortening the space. To enhance the illusion of width, Anne had the floor painted in a black and white diamond pattern. To

ABOVE AND LEFT: The Oriental rug brings together the three elements of the color palette. Red and white upholstery defines one seating area, while blues dominate in a second area, adjacent to the red kitchen. OPPOSITE: The patriotic color scheme repeats in Anne Kinder's folk art and accessories. Using a darker shade of blue for accents punctuates the scheme.

To make the long galley-style kitchen feel shorter, Anne papered the end wall with stripes, which seem to advance. The diamond-pattern flooring makes the space seem wider because the eye travels along the diagonal lines instead of straight across the room.

Q. HOW DO I CONNECT ROOMS WITH COLOR?

keep the cabinets from appearing to float on the wall, the architect anchored them visually with a shelf (not shown), which also adds display space for Anne's collections. Creamy trim and a cameo-color countertop keep the red from overpowering the space.

The same creamy white outlines the walls, windows, and doors in the entry and living-dining area as well, leading the eye from one space to the next. It's important that the wall colors in these adjoining spaces be of equal intensity so they balance visually. In the upholstery, rugs, and accessories, however, the color scheme plays out in a range of tones, from powdery blue to navy and from berry to rust and true red to create variety and interest.

OPTION 5 PLAY WITH THE LIGHT.

It's a simple fact that light changes the appearance of any given color. Take the same can of yellow paint and apply it to two rooms, one that receives little natural light and another that's flooded with sunshine, and it will look like two different colors. To achieve a feeling of continuity and still give each room a subtly different feeling, exaggerate this effect: Choose two closely related hues and apply the lighter one to the sunniest space. This works well for L-shape rooms, where one leg of the L is the living area and one leg the dining area. In the cottage on pages 26–27, the dining area doubles as a passageway from the living room at the front of the house to the den at the

TILE COLORS Your socks should match, but tiles don't have to. Tiles come in a more limited range of colors than do wall paints and wallpapers, but you don't need to worry about matching the two exactly. Anne's red tiles are not identical to the red she mixed for her walls, but the intervening white tiles that frame the red ones make the red appear brighter and help fool the eye into assuming that the reds match. To make sure all your tiles match each other, buy all you'll need from the same lot number.

Q. HOW DO I CONNECT ROOMS WITH COLOR?

BELOW AND OPPOSITE: Keeping colors closely related gives each room a slightly different feeling—cozy in the den, airy in the dining room—yet provides for seamless flow. BELOW RIGHT: Let the architecture be your guide in determining where to stop one color and start another. A white pilaster (half-column) marks the transition from the den wall to that of the dining area, but the soffit between the pilaster and column could match either room color, depending on whether you want to emphasize the connection to the den or to the dining area.

back, so it's important that color appear continuous. Two half-walls with columns and a chair rail on the wall between them help define the dining area. A parchment color applied in the den appears pale yellow when the morning sun pours in, but by the afternoon, the room is in shadow, so it appears cozier and more neutral in color. The dining area and living room, however, receive light from a skylight as well as from the south and west, so the spaces are light-filled throughout the day. To play up the natural illumination, the walls in these areas are a shade of yellow that's slightly lighter than the parchment, imbuing the rooms with a sunny feeling all day long. White trim throughout guarantees a bright, fresh effect.

COLOR CONCEPTS
COLOR THEORY

The color wheel offers the easiest way to visualize how hues relate to each other. Traditionally, artists have defined red, yellow, and blue as the three primary colors from which all others on the wheel can be mixed. Although this is technically true, an artist can't actually derive a pure green or purple from the primaries—the intensity of the mixed color won't equal that of the parents. For decorating decisions, however, you need only be aware that purple relates to both red and blue and that green derives from yellow and blue. Those relationships mean the colors will harmonize with each other.

COLOR SCHEMES Colors that lie opposite each other on the wheel are complementary; when paired, each makes the other appear more vivid. Those that lie beside each other are analogous; they always look good together because they share a common hue. Triads, or any three equally spaced colors, yield a lively yet balanced combination, but the scheme may feel a little jarring unless you let one color dominate and use the other two as accents.

WARM AND COOL The wheel also helps you identify warm and cool hues. Half the wheel, from red to yellow-green, is considered warm, stimulating, and advancing. Such a description reflects emotional associations (the sun looks yellow, and fire

is orange and red, for example), but it has a basis in physiology: The eye can't bring the red and purple ends of the spectrum into focus at the same time, so it perceives red to be nearer or advancing. The other half of the wheel is described as cool; these colors appear to recede. A warm color scheme needs a dollop of a cool hue to feel well-rounded and complete; a cool scheme needs a jolt of warmth to liven it up. Green and purple may seem to advance or recede, depending on the context; for that reason, some interior designers consider them neutrals that can go with any color.

READING THE WHEEL The wheel *opposite* shows not only the pure hues (the third ring from the center) but also a few of the tints (lighter values) and tones (darker values) of these colors. In decorating, you're more likely to be dealing with tints and tones than with pure hues (peach instead of orange, for example).

You know the formula by heart: Warm colors advance and cool colors recede. The advice that usually follows this statement is to paint the walls a cool color if you want a room to seem larger; if you want it to feel smaller, bathe the walls with a warm hue. Unfortunately, it isn't that simple. A bold green or blue can pull the walls around you just as effectively as the warmest red, while a soft yellow can make the walls seem to dissolve, enhancing the sense of space. It's a matter of value—lightness or darkness—and intensity (how saturated or pure a color is) as much as temperature. In general, lighter, paler, or less intense colors will enlarge the apparent space; darker or more intense colors will shrink it. The impact of color on space is also a question of mood. Color affects your mood, which in turn affects your perception

QUESTION 2

HOW CAN I CHANGE THE SENSE OF SPACE?

of a space and your comfort level in it. Remember, too, that neighboring colors affect each other, following the law of simultaneous contrast: If you juxtapose two colors, the eye will perceive them to be as different from each other as possible. Complements—colors that lie directly opposite each other on the color wheel—don't produce these apparent shifts; instead, they intensify each other. If you use red and green in a room together, the red will seem more red and the green will appear more green. Every scheme needs a dollop of contrast to intrigue the eye and to feel balanced and lively. When you work with complements, you automatically have that contrast. An analogous scheme of warm or cool colors will require the addition of an element of the opposite temperature to give the scheme punch.

Walls painted with a faux-leather treatment of mottled red and brown warm this large room and give it intimacy. White on the woodwork and ceiling keeps the strong color in check.

Q. HOW CAN I CHANGE THE SENSE OF SPACE?

OPTION 1 THINK IN TERMS OF LIGHT AND DARK.

Value refers to how light or dark a color is; among all colors, yellow is the lightest value, and purple is the darkest. When you want to alter the sense of space in a room, use low-value (dark) colors to draw the walls around you or high-value (light) colors to push them away. Every color can range from light to dark, so you can use your favorite hue to shrink a room or expand it by choosing the appropriate value. In the bedroom *below*, interior designer Kelly Amen applied a rich

aubergine to the walls, creating a cocoonlike effect. A light-color carpet keeps the walls from becoming overbearing and balances the gray of the raw concrete ceiling (visible in the mirror behind the bed).

OPPOSITE: A vivid rose hue used in varying values bathes this room in an energizing glow. Doses of white in the bedding, drapery, and woodwork balance the rose so it's not overwhelming. BELOW: A series of paintings creates a strong horizontal line that underscores the impression of dark walls enfolding an occupant. The strong, bright hues of the artwork enliven the eggplant-color walls.

To make a space seem larger, choose a light value of any color or opt for white, cream, or pale neutrals. Whites and pastels tend to recede or to evoke an airy, expansive feeling. For the maximum space-enhancing effect, paint the trim to match the walls. When you eliminate contrast between the walls and the architectural features that ordinarily limit and define the room, you increase the apparent size of the space.

White walls and window trim increase the feeling of space in the breakfast area *below*. Because white reflects light, the walls magnify the already generous amount of natural illu-mination the room receives. Choose white carefully, however: A stark or bright white can feel cold and sterile (see Chapter 10 for more on decorating with white). Wood tones on the floor and furniture bring warmth into all-white spaces. Painting the door to the outside green also keeps the room from being bland and sends a visual cue: "This way to the patio."

To make a long, narrow room seem larger, minimize distracting details by paint-ing them out. In the living room *opposite,* the same creamy neutral color was applied to walls, built-in cabinets, brick fireplace, and window frames, creating a smooth envelope of color.

RIGHT: Painting the French doors green empha-sizes this architectural element and the con-nection to the terrace beyond. The chairs repeat the green note to integrate the accent hue into the room. OPPOSITE: Wall-to-wall car-pet brings the light neutral of the ceiling to the floor so that all surfaces reflect light. The color and darker accents come from the Oriental rug and the furnishings.

In decorating, rules are made to be broken. In this diminutive bathroom the obvious space-enhancing solution would be to paint the beaded-board wainscot and walls the same color, but that would diminish the impact of appealing vintage architecture. Painting the wainscot white and the wall above a soft green plays up the architectural feature while creating the illusion of enhanced space: The wainscot suggests a fence or barrier, so a light color on the wall above seems to recede.

Dark walls in a small space evoke a clublike richness. Slate provides subtle tones of purple and green; a decorative painting technique would yield a similar effect. A walnut-stained chest converted into a vanity and a black and silver framed mirror give the room a stately look. Dark walls also could go high-tech with brushed-steel fixtures and accessories.

OPTION 2 USE CONTRAST TO ALTER THE SENSE OF SPACE.

High contrast between a room's walls and its architectural features outlines the room's boundaries and calls attention to its shape and size. If the room is generous, you'll notice the size more; if it's diminutive, you'll be more aware of that too. Furnishings that stand out sharply against the wall color also help define the space more precisely. Ocean blue walls contrast briskly with white woodwork and upholstery, sharpening awareness of the dimensions and limits of the space. A bold golden yellow, on the other hand, blends with gold-color accessories, painted furniture, and white woodwork and upholstery, enlarging the sense of space even though the color is deep and warm.

BELOW AND OPPOSITE: The sense of space provided by wall color is sometimes less important than the mood the colors evoke: Yellow is cheerful; blue is refreshing. If you choose a color that makes you feel good, you're likely to enjoy being in the space regardless of its apparent size.

OPTION 3 CAMOUFLAGE WITH COLOR.

If you're faced with a boxy room that feels boring, try a multicolor palette to change the proportions. To stretch out the living room *above*, two walls are painted a deep sage green and two a bluish lavender; both colors are drawn from the ceramic tiles on the fireplace facing. To warm up the room, the ceiling wears a creamy French vanilla that contains a strong dose of yellow. In this basically cool room, the red sofa makes a bold splash of color to enliven the space and give the room focus.

The square dining room *opposite* is across the hall from the living room *above*, so the red end wall mirrors the color of the sofa. The remaining walls and ceiling glow with yellow. Although both colors

are warm, red advances more aggressively so the space feels more rectangular than square. One dramatic (cool color) painting balances the window and creates a dynamic tension with the wall color, imbuing the space with energy and excitement.

How do you choose a palette for this kind of illusionism? As a general rule, plan on either a warm or an intense color for the wall you wish to bring forward and either a cool or a subdued color for the walls you wish to push apart. In a long, narrow hall, for example, painting the end wall coral and the corridor walls sage can visually shorten the corridor because the coral will advance visually. Conversely, a short hall will seem longer if you paint the end wall a lighter color and the corridor walls a darker one.

For a starting point in choosing specific colors, consider your givens. If a piece of furniture (such as a red sofa) is a focal point, then choose its complement (green) for the nearest wall. The colors will intensify each other and draw the eye toward that part of the room. For the remaining walls, select a light value of a color that appears in other furnishings or in an architectural feature. In the room *opposite,* the lavender wall derives from the fireplace and relates to the striped slipcovers. For the ceiling, decide whether you want to lower or raise it and choose your color accordingly (see Chapter 3).

No matter how effectively you select colors for this kind of space-altering approach, using different hues on each wall and the ceiling breaks up the space and may easily create visual chaos. Decorating with planes of color—changing hues wherever one plane meets another—is an option best suited to those who enjoy the stimulation of lots of color in their environment.

OPPOSITE AND BELOW: Changing colors wherever one plane meets another is one way to alter the apparent shape and size of a room. Use key furnishings or artwork as the starting points for choosing colors.

THE DIVER

OPTION 4 USE COLOR TO DEFINE A LARGE SPACE.

Lofts and new homes with open plans and cathedral ceilings offer similar architectural challenges for homeowners. If your living room, kitchen, and office all share one large, undivided space, can you use more than one color? And if so, where do you stop one color and start the next? The loft shown on these pages offers some ideas.

Interior designer Kelly Amen deployed color to emphasize the vertical dimension of the two-story main living area *opposite* and to lead the eye into and around the space. The concrete supporting columns divide the walls into sections and provide a natural boundary for starting and stopping colors. (In more traditional homes, cased openings, columns, and pilasters provide the dividing lines.)

To develop the palette, Amen started with the homeowner's sofa, rugs, and chair, pulling out colors that would blend rather than match exactly. The colors are all of a similar intensity, muted or grayed rather than saturated, so they work together harmoniously instead of competing with each other. Their arrangement between the concrete columns progresses from the coolest—a grayed lavender at the entry and stair well (see page 44)—to the warmest—a rosy terra-

PLAN AHEAD Kelly Amen advocates developing a color plan for the whole house even if you don't paint all at once. That way, colors will be cohesive and will work together once you complete the job. He starts with 200 color chips and gradually narrows the palette down to a minimum of 10 or 12 colors to use on ceilings and walls. He warns not to judge the impact of a color until you have all of the furniture back in place. "Otherwise, it's like eating a meal half-cooked," he says.

cotta—and then back around to a cooler, mossy green that wraps up over the balcony (see page 44). Using a palette inspired by nature— olive, sand, the colors of leaves, grass, and sky—is one way to ensure that colors will blend rather than match; this creates an effect that's visually engaging yet unified. On the fireplace wall, Amen refrained

LEFT AND OPPOSITE: Muted hues in the love seat and pillows suggested the palette for the living area, where panels of color emphasize the lofty proportions while leading the eye around the space. An inexpensive but useful armoire with iron-grill doors was painted green to blend into the wall beside the fireplace.

from hanging art in the obvious place in order to play up the slender proportions of the fireplace column. An armoire that holds books and stereo equipment was painted green to blend with the walls; it was too useful to discard, but not a favorite piece to focus on.

To adapt this space-defining approach to your home, start with a rug or fabric that offers three or four compatible colors. Include both warm and cool hues and keep them in the same tonal range. (Subdued or muted colors will provide interest and promote a serene mood.) To map out where you'll apply each color, think about creating a sense of movement through successive spaces by arranging the colors from warm to cool or vice versa.

Also consider the light that each space receives. Natural light changes the appearance of any color. In this loft, which is flooded with light from the south, the walls seem to change from terra-cotta to a softer, rosier hue as the sun moves across the sky. To gauge the impact of light on your chosen colors, buy a quart of each color and brush the paint onto large pieces of poster board. Tape the poster board to the walls to observe how the colors change throughout the day and by lamplight. You also can move your test swatches around to see how the color works with furnishings in varying light conditions.

RIGHT: Terra-cotta walls emphasize the patina of an antique Chinese figure. OPPOSITE: Color defines space in this two-story loft, with concrete columns providing the dividing lines. Hues of similar muted intensity are arranged so they increase in warmth from the interior of the apartment (the stair area) toward the exterior. These colors came straight from the can (see page 163 for information). Don't worry about matching fabric and paint colors precisely; blending and harmonizing will achieve a more natural and comfortable result.

COLOR CONCEPTS
VALUE AND INTENSITY

You're probably attracted to colors not only for their specific hue—red, blue-green, orange—but also for particular values of those hues—pink, teal, or terra-cotta, for example. Value refers to the lightness or darkness of a color: Sky blue and robin's-egg blue are light values of blue, while navy and cobalt are dark ones. A hue's value becomes lighter with the addition of white (see the blue and yellow scales *opposite*); black or umber (a blackish brown) darkens the value.

Another aspect of any color is its intensity or saturation. The pure hue represents the most intense or most saturated expression of a color. Adding the hue's complement grays or muddies the color so that it's softer, more muted, and less intense (see the red and green grid *opposite*). Note that each new tone created by mixing doses of opposites with each other can also change in value with the addition of white or black (or umber). Lower-intensity colors (like those shown on pages 42–45) generally create a calm, restrained mood that's subtle and serene.

Higher-intensity (saturated) colors generate more energy and can feel dynamic or richly elegant, depending on the specific colors and the style of your furnishings.

The key to successful color scheming is balance. Strong colors call for strong partners. This applies to both value and intensity. Navy blue walls, for example, demand an equally intense yellow or red to create a balanced scheme. Light and medium values likewise live most comfortably with each other, but to keep a light-value scheme from becoming boring, include an accent of a darker value. In a room decorated in light blue and light yellow, for example, a touch of navy blue or cobalt blue will ground the scheme and give it depth.

Keep intensities equal or nearly equal as well. A saturated red calls for an intense green or yellow-green as a partner; a muted red-orange of lower intensity requires an equally muted yellow-green. Pairing colors of different intensities will create a feeling of being out of balance.

LEFT: Intensity refers to how saturated or pure a color is. These flowers represent red-orange in its purest or most intense form. **RIGHT:** A muted, grayed version of red-orange paints the wall to the right of the sofa and appears in the sofa cushion fabric.

RIGHT AND BELOW RIGHT: Mixing complements changes color intensity. For example, mixing red and green moves the two colors gradually closer to a muted neutral. Adding white lightens the value of each color along the scale. For successful color combinations, keep intensities and values nearly equal.

VALUE

VALUE

INTENSITY

LEFT AND ABOVE LEFT: Value refers to a color's lightness or darkness. Blue is a darker value than yellow, and the scale shows how both blue and yellow can be made lighter in value by adding white. For a balanced color scheme, pair colors of equal value—deep yellow with navy blue or butter yellow with sky blue.

The ceiling represents one-sixth of the space in a room, but too often it gets nothing more than a coat of white paint. In fact, for decades, white has been considered not only the safest but also the best choice for ceilings. There are times when it really is the perfect solution, but if you never consider anything beyond ordinary white, you may be missing an opportunity to add excitement and drama to a room.

What colors should you consider? As a general rule, ceilings that are lighter than the walls feel higher, while those that are darker feel lower. "Lower" need not mean claustrophobic: Visually lowered ceilings can evoke cozy intimacy. As with wall colors, consider the source and strength of light the room receives during the time you're most often using it. Bright daylight bouncing off a blush pink or sky blue

WHAT COLOR SHOULD I PAINT MY CEILING?

ceiling creates an airy feeling; candlelight and lamplight reflecting on tomato red produce a rich glow. Also consider the finish: Ceiling paint is usually flat, but an eggshell or satin paint will offer just a hint of reflective sheen, a benefit if you're using a darker color. Color on the ceiling can enhance a room's character, but beware of excess: Unless you have a very ornate ceiling with intricate moldings, elaborate illusionistic paint techniques are best left to Renaissance palazzi. Soft clouds drifting on a blue sky can be fun for a baby's room or even a bedroom, and a tiny powder room is a good candidate for visual surprises such as cherubs cavorting on the ceiling. For your primary living areas, however, keep the ceiling treatment simple so you don't grow tired of it. After all, you don't want the ceiling to compete for attention with your furnishings or the people in the room.

A shade of white is a good choice for the ceiling when you want to wrap the room in bold color. Cobalt walls feel rich and relaxing when counterbalanced by plenty of white on the floor and ceiling and at the windows.

Q. WHAT COLOR SHOULD I PAINT MY CEILING?

OPTION 1 **WHITE IS THE OBVIOUS CHOICE.**

And sometimes it's the best choice too. White overhead tends to disappear, so your attention focuses on the walls and furnishings. A white ceiling also offsets intense wall color: Boldly colored walls look crisp and sharp, and the ceiling feels higher. If the walls are pale and therefore space-expanding, a white ceiling opens the space even more. Like any other color element in the room, a white ceiling needs an echo, something to help integrate it into the scheme: Woodwork, carpet, draperies, and even bedding can serve the purpose. Otherwise the room will feel out of balance. In rooms that receive scant natural light, a white ceiling helps boost the perceived illumination by reflecting whatever light is available.

Which white is right? The basic ceiling white can look too stark and clinical, but paint companies offer a range of cool and warm

OPPOSITE AND BELOW: When the walls are dark or boldly colored, handsome architectural features, such as deep crown moldings, wainscoting, a mantel, and wide window frames, show up best highlighted with white. A white ceiling balances these elements without calling attention to itself.

whites. Some appear to have a hint of color but look white when paired with a darker wall. Or ask the paint store to tint the basic ceiling white with a touch of your wall color to cut the brightness. In either case, test the color on a sample board before painting.

OPTION 2 BE ADVENTUROUS: TRY A COLOR.

Applying a contrasting color to the ceiling can dramatically alter your perception of the space. It's like a reflector bouncing light down into the room, and the quality of that light affects the room's character. Interior designer Kelly Amen selects glazes that are beautiful in their own right and uses them to create rich effects even in the humblest spaces. In the rooms *opposite* and *right*, the ceilings are the standard 8 feet high and the rooms are small, joined by a cased opening.

Disregarding the rule that low ceilings require a light color, Amen called for a dark green base to be applied to the ceilings, with a glaze of the same color over it. The glaze softens the effect, and the sheen reflects enough light to keep the ceiling from overpowering the room. To give each area its own personality, he had the walls in the dining room painted a pale, minty green and those in the living

ABOVE RIGHT: A cased opening separates the dining room from the living room; the ceiling color connects the two, but each has a different wall color. The woodwork was stripped and waxed, adding a warm neutral accent. OPPOSITE AND RIGHT: Although the ceiling is darker than the walls, a subtle glaze reflects light softly so the space feels quiet and serene. Draperies that fall from the ceiling to the floor create a strong vertical line that helps lift the ceiling visually.

area a barely-there raspberry. A mother-of-pearl glaze over both adds depth. Glazed finishes can be applied to either smooth or textured surfaces, but the texture will yield a different look.

Dark ceilings create shadows, sculpting a simple space to evoke more interest. In the dining room (see page 52), a brightly colored area rug balances the dark ceiling. In the living area (see page 53), the floor is undressed for a clean, uncluttered look that plays up the golden tones of the armoire, coffee table, and bamboo side table. Gossamer draperies of jute rope form soft columns of ethereal color that link the ceiling to the wood floor.

A tiny hall is a transition area that is usually overlooked. Here, turquoise and gold paint combed on the walls and plum applied to the ceiling give the space special character. Door frames and crown molding are painted a warm, glossy white to provide crispness and contrast. OPPOSITE: A faux-parchment finish on the cabinets contrasts with the golden ocher walls, creating depth.

Q. WHAT COLOR SHOULD I PAINT MY CEILING?

If dark ceilings don't suit your style, consider pastels or mid-tones. A hue that's lighter than or equal to the value of the walls will seem to rest lightly on the room. Soft spring green, pale aqua, or light blue floating above warm yellow walls creates a sunny, cheerful effect. Blue or aqua suggests the sky and recalls the Southern tradition of painting porch ceilings light blue to enhance the cooling effect of shade.

How do you decide which colors to use? Let your drapery or upholstery fabric guide you in selecting both wall and ceiling colors, and you'll automatically have a visual link tying the surfaces and furnishings together. Don't worry about matching paint to fabric exactly; if the colors are close, the combination will work. As a general rule, if you want warm color on your walls, choose a cool accent color from the fabric to use on the ceiling. Conversely, if you prefer a cool color

for the walls, apply a tint of a warm color from the fabric to the ceiling. This balancing act keeps the scheme interesting and satisfying.

If you have high ceilings as in the dining room *below*, apply a color to the ceiling and keep the walls nearly white to add drama and warmth while making the most of light. Ecru walls with ivory trim and matching draperies would be too predictable without the tomato bisque ceiling. The hue is drawn from the rug and imparts a pinkish

glow to the room—a flattering light for guests and for food. Use a satin-sheen paint for the ceiling to bounce light down into the room.

OPPOSITE: The fabric at the windows and on the chair pads suggested the choice of light green for the ceiling and warm yellow for the walls in this casual dining area. CENTER: A tomato bisque color on the ceiling picks up a note from the Celtic rug and brings a pinkish glow to the room day and night. BELOW: In a sunny room, pale blue on the ceiling evokes cooling breezes or a summer sky above glowing yellow walls.

Interior designer Kelly Bryant O'Neal painted his kitchen soffit and ceiling beige, then whitewashed them with flat latex paint for a gentler, powdery look. On the wall below the cabinets, he applied a reddish brown paint, then colorwashed it with black. Bored with the look of his old refrigerator, he decoupaged the surface with pages from old books he bought at flea markets.

High ceilings like those found in 1920s Craftsman-style bungalows are good candidates for painting darker than the walls too. If you like a boldly graphic effect, try a high-contrast combination. In the kitchen *at right,* the black ceiling seems to disappear, while the soffits provide a gallerylike backdrop for artwork, a series of paintings of Fiestaware pitchers. Owner and architect Marc Tarasuck added the ceiling beams to hide the new wiring required for track lighting. The light color of the beams echoes the celadon stain on the Douglas fir floors, a detail that helps tie the room together visually. The room's black, yellow, and white combination succeeds because the walls and accessories are bold and bright and the white cabinets provide visual relief. The room would also be handsome, although more subdued, if the walls were periwinkle blue instead of yellow.

If you like a quieter look, choose colors with lower contrast. In the kitchen *opposite,* the ceiling and soffit are a medium-tone beige, the wall cabinets a warm cream, and the base cabinets a dark greenish gray. The base cabinets, previously cobalt blue, received a coat of

PAINTING WITH GRAPHITE Revive old cabinets with this technique. Graphite, available at hardware stores, is normally used to unstick locks. Mixed with clear polyurethane, however, it creates a wonderful tinted finish for woodwork. To avoid bubbles in the liquid, slowly stir graphite, a little at a time, into the polyurethane; the more graphite you add, the darker the finish will be. Sand the cabinets to help the polyurethane adhere better and to smooth the edges of chipped spots. Then brush on the graphite mixture. Use oil-base polyurethane if the paint on the cabinets is oil-base; use water-base polyurethane if the paint is latex.

polyurethane mixed with graphite dust for an updated, hardwearing finish. The terra-cotta tile floor and a red vintage stove accent the neutral scheme. Note that in both of these kitchens, painting the soffit and ceiling the same color brings the eye right to the vintage cabinets. If your kitchen has more wall area, painting the soffit to match the walls (instead of the ceiling) will lead the eye up to the ceiling and increase its apparent height.

Q. WHAT COLOR SHOULD I PAINT MY CEILING?

OPTION 3 PAINT IT THE SAME COLOR AS THE WALLS.

Applying the same hue to walls and ceiling wraps the room in a cloak of color. This approach isn't for everyone—it can make the space feel smaller or more enclosed, because there's no "escape hatch" of lighter color at the top. If the look appeals to you, however, you'll find that in a small room, seamless color evokes a restful, soothing mood, perfect for a bedroom or bath. In a larger room, the one-color treatment unifies the space and focuses attention on the furnishings and accessories that fill it. If a room is oddly shaped and has a multiangled ceiling, carrying the wall color across the ceiling can simplify the shape and unify the space. A same-color ceiling seems lower, so it makes a room with lofty proportions feel more intimate. Applying the same color to walls and ceiling also makes your painting job easier, because you won't have to tape off the molding at the ceiling line.

Whether you show off the crown molding and other trim with a contrasting color or paint them to blend in

RIGHT: A fireplace is the room's natural focal point. Painting the mantel black makes the walls seem lighter by contrast. OPPOSITE: A red base coat on the walls and ceiling was washed with layers of avocado, purple, and gold, applied with sea sponges wrapped in terry cloth, muslin, and nubby cotton rags. To give the bump-out wall around the fireplace subtle texture, copper-color tissue paper was crumpled, then smoothed flat and pasted onto the walls.

depends on your personal preferences. Highlighting the trim accents the architecture the way a good belt sets off a suit. You don't have to treat all trim the same: If the crown molding is small, paint it out, but emphasize the windows with contrasting color for visual relief.

When you apply the same color to walls and ceiling, use the same type of paint for both, for the sake of simplicity and economy. In a bathroom or kitchen, where walls need to be washable, semi-gloss is the usual choice, and its sheen will help bounce light off the ceiling. If you prefer a less glossy finish, try eggshell (sometimes called satin or low-luster paint); it has more shine than flat paint but less than semigloss. In areas where walls aren't as likely to need frequent washing, flat paint works fine and is the best choice for imperfect walls. Glossier finishes will show up every dent, chip, and nick. High-gloss paint is best for woodwork and cabinet doors.

RIGHT: The high ceilings found in older homes are perfect candidates for receiving the same color as the walls, because the color lowers them visually without making the room feel closed in. Here the warm color up top is balanced by white below. The effect is clean and sunny. **OPPOSITE:** Crown molding adds a traditional touch to a contemporary home. With 10-foot ceilings and undressed windows, the room gains warmth and character from the coral pink walls and ceiling. The fireplace surround is faced with 12-inch-square ceramic tile that looks like stone.

POPCORN ANYONE? "Popcorn" ceilings are textured, acoustic surfaces made by spraying the ceiling drywall with a mixture of paint and foam pellets. It's an inexpensive finish for new homes and is sometimes used to cover cracks in older plaster ceilings. Ceilings covered with an acoustic popcorn finish cannot be glazed, because the foam beads come loose and fall off when brushed. If you have this type of ceiling and you wish to color it, prime it and then use flat-finish paint, applying both with a roller that has a fluffy ¾-inch nap.

OPTION 4 LET THE ARCHITECTURE BE YOUR GUIDE.

Vaulted, cathedral, or multiangled ceilings can pose a special problem. Where do you start and stop color? In low attics, carrying the same color across the ceiling from wall to wall is a practical solution. However, you can increase the apparent height of the ceiling with a little visual trickery: Add a chair rail around the wall at about hip height; then paint the area below the chair rail a darker hue than the area above. Hand-painted stripes emphasize the vertical dimension and further tease the eye into perceiving the ceiling as higher than it really is. Because attic rooms often receive natural light through only one or two windows, keep the walls and furnishings light in color to brighten the space. Or, if you want to create a sense of snug retreat, choose muted, darker colors. Or let your furnishings

ABOVE: Adding a chair rail in this attic helped create the illusion of more headroom. A striped paint treatment below the chair rail anchors the room visually. **OPPOSITE** In this attic room, all surfaces are painted a light-reflecting white, and furnishings supply the color.

and accessories provide the color in a white, light-reflecting space.

If you have a cathedral ceiling, don't feel compelled to carry its color all the way to the floor just because there's no crown molding to define the top of the wall. Architectural features, such as molding or timber framing, do make it easier to know where to stop and start color, but wherever one plane or flat surface meets another, you can change colors. You'll need to tape off the ceiling carefully to keep the dividing line sharply defined and straight; an uneven line where the two colors meet will spoil the look.

Changing colors where the wall meets the ceiling will focus attention on the living space instead of on the soaring height of the ceiling. In a room with walls that angle sharply to the ceiling but offer more headspace than traditional attics, extend the wall color onto the angled walls up to the flat part of the ceiling. This will keep the room from feeling cramped. If necessary, add crown molding to define where the walls end and the ceiling begins.

Color need not come only from paint. If you like the look of wood, consider covering the ceiling with wood paneling. Attach the paneling to the ceiling joists as you would to the walls.

If the paint color changed where the walls meet the angled planes, the room would feel cramped—as if you had to stoop to enter. Treating the angled planes as part of the wall allows the eye to travel higher, to the crown molding outlining the ceiling proper. Tucking the bed into the angled space creates a snug retreat, and the bedroom becomes a hideaway.

COLOR CONCEPTS

COLOR AND MOOD

How are the colors you love going to make you feel once you get them on the walls, the floor, and the furniture?

RED has been shown to raise blood pressure and speed respiration and heart rate. Because it increases appetite and heightens the sense of taste and smell, red is a good choice for dining rooms. It is usually considered too stimulating for bedrooms, but if you're only in the room after dark, you'll be seeing it mostly by lamplight, when the color will appear muted, rich, and elegant. Crimson can make some people feel irritable; if you love red but it bugs your mate, try small touches in accessories or upholstery fabrics.

BLUE brings down blood pressure and slows respiration and heart rate. That's why it's considered calming, relaxing, and serene and is often recommended for bedrooms and bathrooms. Be careful, however: A pastel blue that looks pretty on the paint chip can come across as unpleasantly chilly when it's on the walls and furnishings, especially in a room that receives little natural light. If you opt for a light blue as the primary color in a room, balance it with warm hues in the furnishings and fabrics. To encourage relaxation in the rooms where people gather—family rooms, living rooms, large kitchens—consider warmer blues, such as periwinkle, or bright blues, such as cerulean or turquoise.

GREEN is considered the most restful color for the eye. Combining the refreshing quality of blue and the cheerfulness of yellow, green is suited to almost any room in the house. In a kitchen, a sage or medium green cools things down; in a family room or living room, it encourages unwinding but has enough warmth to promote comfort and togetherness. In a bedroom, it's relaxing and pleasant.

YELLOW captures the joy of sunshine and communicates happiness. It's perfect for kitchens, dining rooms, and bathrooms, where happy color is energizing and uplifting. In halls, entries, and small spaces, yellow can feel expansive and welcoming.

ORANGE, like red, stimulates appetites. In its pure form, however, orange may be a difficult color to live with. Terra-cotta, salmon, peach, coral, and shrimp are more popular expressions of the hue. Peach is nurturing yet restful in a bedroom; in a bathroom, it flatters light skin tones. Orange shades imbue a living room or family room with warmth and energy. In a kitchen that faces west, however, orange tones may feel unpleasantly hot.

PURPLE in its darkest values (eggplant, for example) is rich, dramatic, and sophisticated. It's associated with luxury as well as creativity, and as an accent or secondary color, it gives a scheme depth. Lighter versions of purple, such as lavender and lilac, bring the same restful quality to bedrooms as blue does, but without the risk of feeling chilly.

NEUTRALS (black, gray, white, and brown) are basic to the decorator's tool kit. All-neutral schemes fall in and out of fashion, but their virtue lies in their flexibility: Add color to liven things up; subtract it to calm things down. Black is best used in small doses as an accent—indeed, some experts maintain that every room needs a touch of black to ground the color scheme and give it depth. For more on white, see Chapter 10.

ENERGIZING

CREATIVE

TRANQUIL

STIMULATING

RELAXING

CHEERFUL

Molding or trim helps define a room's style, adding architectural character and dimension to the walls. Window and door molding and baseboards also serve the practical purpose of concealing the gaps that exist in most houses. Chair rails originally protected plaster walls from nicks when chairs and furniture were pushed against them. Today they're often installed to help alter the apparent height of a wall as much as to protect it from damage.

As a rule, paint all the trim throughout the house the same color to create a unified effect from room to room. Within a room, paint all of the trim the same unless you wish to emphasize elements—a salvaged antique mantel might be left stripped and unstained, for example, while the baseboard, crown molding, door frames, and window frames

QUESTION 4

SHOULD THE TRIM ALWAYS BE WHITE?

are all painted creamy white. Or, to play up a marble or stone mantel, you may choose to paint the baseboards a similar color but paint all window and door frames white.

Before investing in enough paint for the job, buy a quart and test it on a piece of poster board. Place this board beside a test board of the wall color to see how they look together. For doors, window frames, and door frames, choose a gloss or semigloss enamel rather than flat-finish paint; the glossier paint is more durable, and its reflective quality plays up light and shadows. If you're painting over old gloss paint, you'll need to scuff the surface with sandpaper to help the paint adhere better. Alternatively, you can prime the woodwork with a deglossing primer that eliminates the need for sanding.

Highlighted with creamy white, the wainscot, door frames, window frames, and crown molding (not shown) stand out briskly against red walls. Instead of highlighting the molding panels on the walls, however, interior designer Laura Miller painted them to blend in; they add dimension without breaking up the envelope of color that enlarges the sense of space. Previous owners had filled each panel with wallpaper, which made the room feel busier and more formal.

Q. SHOULD THE TRIM ALWAYS BE WHITE?

OPTION 1 **FOR CRISPNESS AND RELIABLE GOOD LOOKS, YES.**
If your walls wear a color, whether soft or bold, then white trim is practically guaranteed to set them off well. In rooms with dark or intensely colored walls, white lightens and brightens, accenting the strong hue and bringing visual relief. In rooms with light or pastel walls, white trim makes the color look cleaner and clearer while introducing a mere hint of contrast. Remember that white trim does

not mean stark white—most paint manufacturers offer a range of whites that go from warm to cool. Also, the lightest shade on a paint card may function as a white when juxtaposed with your wall color.

How do you choose a white for your trim? Start with the paint chip of your wall color and hold it up to a variety of white or pale neutral chips to see which ones you like. Warm creamy tones pair well with warm or intense colors and warm neutrals, while clear or

OPPOSITE AND BELOW: Whether the walls are an energizing, warm color, such as terra-cotta, or a serene, cool hue, such as pale green, white trim keeps the room feeling airy and light-filled. In the morning room, curtains made of scrim, washed to shrink and crinkle it, soften the windows without blocking light. (Look for scrim in the drapery and upholstery section of fabric stores.)

Deep baseboards and wide molding around double-hung windows characterize many homes built before the 1940s. Originally the woodwork probably would have been stained a medium brown or golden tone, but painting it white freshens and updates the room and makes the yellow walls look brighter.

cool whites make good partners for cool colors, both saturated and muted.

OPTION 2 DEFINE WITH COLOR.

Painting the woodwork darker than the walls focuses attention on window and door frames. If you love color, consider painting the trim a contrasting hue that's equal in intensity to the wall color. The profusion of happy color in the Tudor-style house *at right* was inspired by the painted cupboard and a collection of Fiestaware under the window. Window fabric, favorite dinnerware, and majolica are good sources for colors too.

Choose the lightest or brightest hue for the major surfaces, a darker color for the window and door frames, and a third, medium tone for window sashes and skirting boards (the board under the windowsill). The two-color window treatment draws attention to interesting windows as well as the view.

If the architecture of your house is formal and traditional, painting the baseboards to mimic marble can impart a look of grandeur. Because it's visually heavy

RIGHT: Cheerful color transforms the kitchen: White laminate cabinets were sprayed golden-yellow, with dark green detailing on the side panels, toe-kick, and trim. Yellow paint and a soft brown glaze blend the brick wall with the cupboards and remaining walls.

MAKE YOUR OWN MARBLE In a house with traditional architectural details, marble baseboards and floors add a sophisticated elegance. Look in the Yellow Pages under "Paint Contractors" to find professional decorative painters. Or, if you have an artistic bent (and patience), do the job yourself. If you've never tried marbleizing, practice on a small project first, using a kit from a crafts store. Home improvement centers will have the supplies you need to work on a larger scale. Use semigloss latex paints. You'll need a base color, one or two top colors, glazing medium, and a high-contrast color for the veins. Apply the base color and let it dry. Mix the glaze with one top color (about 1 part paint to 4 parts glaze) and sponge it over the base coat, allowing some of the base to show. After the glaze dries, repeat with the second top color. Then mix the glaze with the veining color and drag it in diagonal lines with a feather (turkey feathers, also available at crafts stores, work best).

(and you're imitating stone), this specialty treatment is most effective if you limit it to the baseboards, floors, stair risers, and mantels. If you apply it to door and window frames as well, the overall effect may be too dark and weighty. A coat of white on these surfaces keeps the look fresh.

If walls are white or cream, contrasting crown molding and baseboards outline the room's dimensions. Around windows, the darker trim frames the view to the outdoors the way a mat frames a picture. Off-white or cream walls with contrasting trim—gray-blue, muted green, mustard yellow, or barn red, for example—recall colonial-style interiors and have long been a favorite for collectors of country antiques and furnishings. White limewashed walls were an economical choice for 18th-century homeowners, because pigments were

OPPOSITE: If your walls are a pale color, you can emphasize windows, doors, and other architectural features by painting them with a soft, contrasting hue. ABOVE: Interior designer Kelly Bryant O'Neal revitalized the old molding in his 1928 cottage with gold leaf and jazzed up the French doors with bright pea green paint. Keeping the window and door frames white enlivens the wall color but lets the French doors and molding take the spotlight.

Q. SHOULD THE TRIM ALWAYS BE WHITE?

scarce and expensive. Now they provide a clean backdrop for the honeyed tones of old wood. Painted trim, which disguised inexpensive wood in the 18th century, brings color into the room today.

Because darker trim against light walls calls so much attention to the woodwork, consider whether your woodwork is worth the notice. Baseboards measuring about 6 inches deep and crown molding 3 to 4¼ inches deep have enough substance to make an impact. Simple, ranch-style moldings weren't originally intended to be focal points;

their modest proportions and utilitarian character are best served with a stained finish or a color lighter than or the same as the walls.

BELOW LEFT AND RIGHT: Soft green trim outlining windows and bookcases accents the architecture while preserving the sense of soaring space. The color continues around the room in narrow bands that emphasize the horizontal dimension and give the room a more human scale. OPPOSITE: Painting out the trim around the door to the bathroom minimizes contrast and emphasizes an envelope of color; for the door leading to the rest of the house, a high-contrast white sends a subconscious signal: "This way out."

Q. SHOULD THE TRIM ALWAYS BE WHITE?

OPTION 3 STAINED WOOD PLAYS UP NATURAL TEXTURE.
Homes that were built in the late 1800s and early 1900s, particularly in the Victorian and Arts and Crafts styles, featured a wealth of oak woodwork stained or varnished to produce a medium brown or honey gold. Ranch-style houses built in the 1950s and 1960s featured simpler, narrower moldings, but the unpainted look still prevailed. Leaving the trim and doors a natural color plays up the beautiful texture of wood and brings warmth to interiors. The color impact on your rooms will depend on whether you only varnish the wood (which doesn't significantly alter the natural hue) or stain first.

Stain contains dyes or pigments that will color the wood without hiding the grain. A full range of colors is available, from pickled or bleached to golden yellow, reddish brown, dark brown, and ebony. Bleached or pickled woodwork will have a modern-country look, while the golden and medium brown tones will confirm an Arts and Crafts or Mission style. Ebony is dramatic for floors and doors in a contemporary setting. Whichever you choose, think in terms of color rather than type of wood in order to achieve the effect you want in your home.

RIGHT: The medium-brown color of stained and varnished wood in the living room tones down the brilliance of the yellow walls. The same wall color continues into the adjoining room, where white trim creates a brighter, crisper look.
OPPOSITE: Yellow and orange tones in the woodwork and sideboard provide a warm foil for soft green walls in this analogous scheme. If you think of wood in terms of its stain color, then the color wheel can guide you toward happy pairings.

STRIPPING WOODWORK If your woodwork's finish is scratched and flaking, or if it's a darker stain than you like, apply a commercial stripper labeled for varnish and stain. If you're working on vertical surfaces, look for a gel stripper; it won't run down the frame the way liquid stripper will. Follow the manufacturer's directions. You can lighten the stripped wood somewhat with bleach, but the original stain will have penetrated the grain and darkened it permanently. Apply the new color of stain according to the manufacturer's instructions; follow with varnish to seal and protect the wood.

Q. SHOULD THE TRIM ALWAYS BE WHITE?

If you're starting from scratch, use stain-grade molding; paint-grade molding is composed of short lengths glued together, so the stain or varnish will emphasize the joints and may be absorbed unevenly. Test the stain on the edges of a door or the back of molding to see if you like the color; the way it reacts to your wood may not match the store sample.

Wood that has already been stained and varnished may only need to be cleaned with a liquid furniture cleaner in order to look fresher. If you need to revarnish, clean the woodwork with denatured alcohol, then sand carefully using 180-grit sandpaper. (Sand with the grain.) Use a rag dampened with denatured alcohol to wipe off the sanding dust. Then let the surface dry completely before brushing on new varnish.

If your woodwork is painted and you want to return to a natural finish, be prepared for a painstaking project. You'll need to apply a peel-and-strip paste with a trowel, cover it with plastic sheeting (which comes with the stripper), and let it work for several hours. When you peel away the plastic, the paint and paste should come off together. This technique is intended to mitigate problems with lead paint, but if you have a big project with lots of lead paint, you may need to remove the trim to have it stripped professionally or have professionals come into your home to tackle the job.

RIGHT AND OPPOSITE: Choose your stain color according to the look you want: Medium to dark brown stain creates a visually heavier feeling, while lighter, golden or honey-toned stains can appear nearly as sunny as a yellow wall. Using stain (instead of paint) takes advantage of the grain of the wood and brings natural texture to the room.

Like the ceiling, the floor is one-sixth of a room's surface area, so the floor covering has a major impact on the color personality of the space. It can help create an air of comfort and luxury—or it can make you want to climb the walls. If you move into a house with carpet in place and it's not a color or texture you like, what are your options? Carpet laid over hardwood floors that are in good condition is easy to pull up with a crowbar and the help of a few friends. But if the carpet lies over subflooring and your budget doesn't allow for replacing it right away, you have a couple of choices for downplaying its impact. One is to use the carpet as a starting point for developing a new color scheme more to your liking. Fabric is your friend here. A multicolor print or floral that includes the carpet color as an accent will establish

QUESTION 5

I CAN'T CHANGE MY CARPET. WHAT SHOULD I DO?

a new color theme for the room while incorporating the carpet. This works particularly well in bedrooms, where bedding and draperies can quickly transform the room's appearance. Another option is to layer a large area rug or several smaller rugs over the carpet. You can also layer smaller area rugs over room-size rugs to define conversation areas or to give focus to a room. In the room *opposite*, the larger rug brings the pale neutral of the ceiling and walls to the floor, creating an open, airy feeling. By itself, however, it leaves the seating pieces floating in the light-color space. Centering a brick red Oriental rug on top immediately warms the space and anchors the room visually. Shifting the color scheme or layering rugs can resolve many carpet problems. Sometimes, however, replacement is really the only happy solution.

Layering a smaller rug over a room-size rug or wall-to-wall carpeting draws the eye to the conversation area and changes the color emphasis of a room.

Q. I CAN'T CHANGE MY CARPET. WHAT SHOULD I DO?

OPTION 1 **COVER IT UP.**

The easiest way to deal with an unwanted carpet you can't change is to cover it up. A room-size area rug will cover enough of the offending carpeting to minimize its color effect. Even a smaller rug can help change the room's personality if the rug is centered over the most prominent part of the room. The underlying carpet becomes a bor- der for the area rug, and its impact on the room is minimized. In the living room or family room, position the rug to define the primary conversational grouping. In a bedroom, cover the area around the bed, using several rugs if necessary. To keep the smaller rug from "creeping" or bunching on top of the wall-to-wall carpeting, use a double-stick carpet pad under it.

The living room *below* illustrates what a difference a rug can make. The existing floor covering, *opposite,* is low-pile blue-green wall-to-wall carpet that isn't obnoxious but does clamor for attention and exert a cooling influence over the room. To cozy things up, a large-patterned area rug can be centered under the conversational grouping, *center.* The rug's border incorporates patches of the carpet color and a salmon pink, which harmonizes with the rust-colored upholstered chairs. For a more neutral look, *below,* sisal or a wool rug that simulates the color and texture of sisal can be layered over the carpeting. The effect is clean, casual, and warm, and the rust brown upholstered chairs become the deepest tone in a sunny, honey-hued room.

OPTION 2 SHIFT THE COLOR SCHEME IN A NEW DIRECTION.

When carpeting is in good condition, use it as a starting point to develop a new look. Shop for fabrics that pick up your given hue but move the room's overall palette in a new direction. Slipcovers, draperies, bedding, and paint will completely change the room's mood.

To begin developing a new scheme, look at a color wheel (see page 29) to see which hues are likely to work. Don't limit yourself to the color wheel, however. Also keep an eye out for your given color in magazines, catalogs, even decorative objects—you may see it in an unexpected pairing that can inspire a pleasing new palette.

In the bedroom *below right,* for example, the homeowners had originally installed silver-blue carpet like that used throughout the house. Uncertain about what to do with the walls, they left them white and dressed the bed with yellow and blue bedding. Seven years later, they were tired of the white walls and blue carpet. They wanted something more dramatic, but a new floor covering wasn't in the budget. A catalog photograph showing powder blue dinnerware atop cocoa brown cloth bags sparked the idea for the new color scheme shown *at left.*

LEFT AND RIGHT: Changing the wall color and bedding changes the carpet's impact. When the walls were white and the bedding yellow, the carpet seemed more blue. With a new, neutral scheme, the carpet appears more neutral too. If dark walls seem too risky, remember that lighter bedding will balance them. And furniture that's even deeper in hue ensures that the walls aren't the darkest element, so they won't overwhelm you.

BEFORE

WHAT COLOR FOR THE CARPET? Neutral carpet may seem like the safest, most versatile choice—the floor's equivalent to white walls—but unlike the walls, the carpet has to camouflage dirt and wear from constant traffic. Patterned carpets and those with multicolor fibers hide dirt better than solid-color carpets do. A floor covering that's darker than the walls grounds the room because the visually heaviest element is at the bottom. Carpet that's lighter will expand the sense of space; to balance the flooring, keep the ceiling light too.

Q. I CAN'T CHANGE MY CARPET. WHAT SHOULD I DO?

If you find a source of inspiration in a catalog photo, fabric scrap, or piece of china, take it to the paint store and look for paint chips that are similar in hue. Bring them home and lay them on the carpet to see which you like best. Then test a quart of your favorite on a piece of poster board to get a better idea of how it will look in the room.

Next, look for draperies and bedding that relate to the new wall color and that include the carpet color as an accent. In the bedroom *opposite,* fabrics in an array of cocoa browns, tans, and beiges include touches of silver-blue. The fabrics don't have to match either the carpet or the wall color exactly; if the hues are similar and include a range of tones from light to dark, you'll have a more interesting mix and the fabrics will bridge the difference between the new wall color and the old carpet color.

CUSTOM BEDDING If you can't find ready-made bedding in the colors you want, consider buying decorator fabrics and making your own or having someone do the job for you. Duvet covers, pillow shams, and bedskirts aren't difficult to make, although handling the large amounts of fabric required can be awkward. If you have intermediate sewing skills, you can make your own goblet-pleat draperies; or purchase plain tab-top curtains and add an edging of fabric that coordinates with your bedding. Choose at least one each of a large-scale print, a medium-scale design, and a small print. The easiest way to create a coordinated ensemble is to work with decorator fabric collections. Check fabric stores or order fabric online (for more information, see page 164).

ARTFUL ARRANGEMENTS To create a display of plates, first trace them onto paper and cut out the shapes. Tape the shapes to the wall to determine the best arrangement. Then place the plate (mounted in its picture hanger) on the shape and mark the position for the nail. Hammer the nail through the paper pattern; tear away the paper and hang the plate.

RIGHT: Simple goblet-pleat draperies filter the light. When you choose drapery hardware, keep the proportions of the room and the window in mind: A tray ceiling (see page 88) lends a sense of loftiness to this room, and the picture window is nearly 6 feet wide, so the drapery rod needs to be weighty in order to make an impact. OPPOSITE: The bed is the natural focal point of the bedroom, so the wall over the headboard is a perfect spot for displaying artwork or a favorite collection. Brown transferware plates and casserole lids underscore this room's new color scheme.

Another way to draw the eye away from an unloved carpet is to paint the walls a color that lies on the same side of the color wheel as the carpet. These walls were originally pink, and the contrast made the carpet more noticeable. A pale green that leans toward the blue side of the color wheel updates the walls, and new bedding and draperies introduce a fresh scheme. The touches of lighter blue in the comforter and curtains help integrate the floor covering into the new look.

The pink and white striped wallpaper in the bathroom still works with the green. The walk-in closet beyond could have been left its original solid pink, but painting it to match the bedroom sets up a pleasing rhythm that emphasizes the bath as a separate area. White trim unifies all three spaces, and off-white paint revives an old brown bookcase so that it matches the bedside table and cast-iron bed. If the homeowners later decide to replace the carpet with a neutral shade, this color scheme will still succeed.

OPTION 3 **SOMETIMES YOU HAVE TO REPLACE THE CARPET.**
If your floors are covered with burnt orange shag from the 1970s but you really love lavender and periwinkle blue, there's just no happy compromise. You'll have to replace the carpet.

Broadloom or wall-to-wall carpets come in a wide variety of colors, textures, and patterns. To narrow your choices, first consider how much impact you want the floor to have on the room's color scheme. Spreading color underfoot limits the range of hues you can introduce on the walls and in the furnishings (that's what created this decorating problem in the first place), but light or muted tones, such as pale gray-blue or sage green, can actually be fairly versatile. To choose a color for wall-to-wall carpeting, look for a hue that appears in your upholstery or draperies; select a darker shade to make the room feel cozier or a lighter one to open up the space. In a west- or south-facing room, a warm color could make the room feel too hot; a cooler hue offers a more refreshing choice.

A carpet that combines color and pattern stamps a room with strong personality. An orderly grid of medallions, for example, or a repeating pattern of a tapestrylike design suggests a mind-your-manners formality, while a plaid evokes clublike comfort or a sporty, casual atmosphere. Florals may be formal or informal, depending on the

RIGHT: A pale-color cut-pile carpet helps make the room appear more spacious, while a darker color (such as the spruce sample *opposite*) enhances a cozy feeling. The blue sample would help cool down a south- or west-facing room, while the rosy quartz would warm up a north-facing room.

MAGIC CARPET Wool carpet is the most expensive you can buy, but for the best stain resistance and durability, opt for nylon. If you prefer the look and comfort of wool but need the superior stain-repelling quality of nylon, shop for a blend (80 percent wool and 20 percent nylon); blends are more affordable than pure wool but more expensive than pure nylon. For a slightly lower price (and somewhat lower durability), opt for polyester carpeting. Polyester is soft and colorfast, but it doesn't wear as well as nylon, so it's better for areas that receive less traffic and hard use. Olefin, primarily used in basements and on porches, is colorfast and repels water and stains. Invest in a good carpet pad too. A quality pad provides softness and insulation and prolongs the carpet's life. Thicker isn't necessarily better, though: A sink-in pad actually makes a carpet wear out faster if the floor covering is exposed to certain kinds of traffic, such as high heels. Pads should be no thicker than $7/16$ inch.

design. If you have children and pets, patterned carpet may be your best choice, because the pattern helps hide spills and stains.

When you consider patterns, keep your room size as well as furnishings in mind. In a small room, a large repeat won't show to best advantage and can appear overwhelming. Solid furniture (such as bookcases or skirted sofas, chairs, and ottomans) will also hide much of the pattern. Check the pattern repeat against the size and layout of your room to determine whether at least 8 to 10 motifs will show.

If you don't want to commit to a color, choose a neutral. A light neutral makes a room feel more spacious and lets your attention

focus on the furnishings rather than the floor. Neutrals that include specks of dark brown or taupe (such as berbers or their look-alikes) work well in high-traffic areas and don't show dirt.

Along with color and pattern, texture helps define the character a carpet brings to a room. Texture depends on construction. Most wall-to-wall carpets are made by tufting, a process in which machines with long rows of needles embed fiber clusters into a backing material. If both ends of the tuft are stitched to the backing, the result is a loop pile; if the tufts are cut so they stand straight up, the result is a cut-pile carpet.

Q. I CAN'T CHANGE MY CARPET. WHAT SHOULD I DO?

Cut pile may be saxony or plush. Saxony is the most popular; plush is deeper and more luxurious (and more expensive). Both create a uniform swath of color across the floor. Loop pile may be level or multilevel; both are particularly durable and resistant to dirt. Cut-and-loop pile combines both types of surfaces. It doesn't show wear, which makes it a good choice for family rooms and high-traffic areas.

Regardless of which pile you choose, ask the carpet store to let you borrow a large sample to bring home. Like paint, carpet colors seen by daylight or lamplight can look entirely different from the way they appear in the store's fluorescent light. If you're considering buying a patterned carpet, seeing a sample in the room will help you determine whether the scale is right.

OPPOSITE: Whether you choose organic patterns or tidy grids, keep the size of the pattern in scale with your room. At least eight repeats of the motif will need to show to establish the rhythm. BELOW: Textured carpet in neutral colors offers pleasing contrast to the smooth surfaces of walls, tables, and shelves, yet it doesn't distract the eye from fabrics and furnishings.

COLOR CONCEPTS
SEASONAL CHANGE

A few simple color changes can cozy up your rooms for winter and refresh them for spring. In winter, dark, warm colors and rich patterns create an inviting intimacy. The "Winter" living room *opposite bottom* is anchored by a densely patterned red rug. Upholstered chairs wear bold floral and leaf designs, and the sofa pillows sport dark paisleys. A spicy apricot fabric covers the ottoman, which doubles as a coffee table. (For the holidays, a red plaid cover slips over the ottoman.) A black lampshade punctuates the color scheme. On the mantel, architectural prints are layered with dark-colored objects to create visual richness and depth, enhancing the sense of warmth.

To infuse the room with a breath of fresh air for summer, the red carpet comes up, replaced by a light-color area rug. White slipcovers dress the chairs, and a leaf-patterned fabric topper slips on over the ottoman. Floral pillows replace the paisley ones. Shelves and tabletops are cleared to make room for pared down displays of artwork that capture spring and summer themes. A wheat-toned lampshade substitutes for the black one to give the summer scheme a lift.

Seasonal change in the bedroom is even easier, because bedding and window treatments make such an impact on the room. For summer, think light and sunny. Crisp white sheets and a pale yellow summer quilt give the bed a cool, welcoming look, and vintage dresser scarves draped over curtain rods let in summer breezes. For winter, darker colors and rustic textures evoke snuggle-in warmth. Cloak an upholstered chair with a wool coverlet, or stitch up a slipcover in cuddly wool flannel plaid. Bring in woodsy accessories such as pinecones and grapevine wreaths for comforting earthy color. Dress the windows with dark velvet or burlap panels, or substitute a heavier light-color fabric—here, an antique matelassé bedspread hangs over a curtain rod, filtering light without blocking it entirely.

HOLIDAY

SUMMER

WINTER

SUMMER

WINTER

SUMMER

Upholstery and draperies are among the biggest investments in decorating. Paint, on the other hand, is relatively inexpensive and transforms a room more quickly than anything else you can do. (For about $80, you can refresh an average-size family room—that's two coats of paint in an 18x15-foot family room with an 8-foot ceiling.) To make a change, let your fabric be your guide. In fact, this is a good approach to take even if you're starting from scratch. Fabric, carpeting, and tile are available in a more limited range of colors than is paint, so choose them first and then decide on your paint color.

Any fabric can suggest at least three options for wall colors, each of which will produce a different feeling in the room. On the pages that follow, you'll see examples that illustrate this. Once you identify

I LOVE MY SOFA. WHAT COLOR DO I PAINT MY WALLS?

the options your fabric offers, decide which one creates the mood you want to evoke—cozy, calm, relaxed, energetic, playful? Emotional responses to colors vary from person to person, and if you need to please family members as well as yourself, color choices may require some conferences and compromises. Research indicates that people generally perceive warm hues (reds and yellows) as active and stimulating and cool hues (blues and greens) as relaxing. But the intensity or strength of the color can alter those effects. For more about how color influences the mood of a room, see pages 68–69.

Of course, starting with the fabric works for any room in the house, not just a room with a sofa. Bedding and draperies provide easy starting points for adding color to bedrooms and adjoining baths, and even in a powder room, the window treatment can suggest an exciting wall color.

The floral on the sofa points toward at least five possibilities for the room's color scheme: yellow, rose, lavender, green, or cream. Pulling out the soft green of the foliage creates a comfortable, classic cottage look.

Q. I LOVE MY SOFA. WHAT COLOR DO I PAINT MY WALLS?

OPTION 1 CHOOSE A COLOR IN THE FABRIC.

The living rooms shown on these and the following pages were set up in a photo studio to show what a difference you can make in a room simply by changing the wall color. A blue and yellow floral on an off-white background suggests at least three paths for a new color scheme: a midtone blue, a soft green, and a sunny yellow. Each creates a different mood, from tranquil to relaxed to cheerful. For a more dramatic look, a darker green or a darker blue could have been used; however, these shades would also create a heavier feeling that could be too weighty for this garden-room look.

To use your fabric as a starting point, take a pillow or cushion cover from your dominant upholstered piece to the paint store and look for paint chips that pull out the different hues in the fabric. The paint color doesn't have to match the fabric exactly—in fact, if the

wall color is slightly lighter or slightly darker than the color in the fabric, the results will seem "evolved" but harmonious. The major exception is if you want to create the effect shown on pages 7–11, where the wall color and draperies match exactly. This approach enlarges the sense of space in the room by creating an unbroken envelope of color while softening the walls with dimension and depth. To match a solid-color fabric exactly, take a swatch to the paint store or home improvement center; there, a spectrometer, which measures heat and light to determine color, can translate the fabric hue into a formula

OPPOSITE: A blue and yellow floral with an off-white background suggests at least three color options for the walls. Blue is cool and calm but might be too chilly in a north-facing room. CENTER: Green, inspired by the foliage in the fabric, is relaxing yet warm. BELOW: Yellow is sunny and cheerful but might feel too hot in a south-facing room. To use yellow in a room that receives a lot of sun, consider choosing a light creamy shade.

I LOVE MY SOFA. WHAT COLOR DO I PAINT MY WALLS ?

for matching paint. This only works on solid fabric, however. Any variations in tone will prevent the machine from reading the color.

Even a stripe with subtle color variations can point to a variety of combinations. The sofa fabric shown *below* includes deep rose, ivory, and two shades of tan. Any of these could suggest a paint color for the walls. The lighter value is somewhat bland in this instance *(below)*, while the darker tones offer a richer effect.

Choosing a darker tone for the walls makes light-color upholstery pop by contrast, creating a more dramatic environment. If the draperies match the paint or are close to the same shade, the walls and draperies work together to form a consistent background, against which the sofa stands out as the focal point. If you choose a lighter value for the draperies, then the darker wall color will draw more attention to the windows.

As you narrow your choices, remember that a color that looks dark on the paint chip will seem even darker on the walls. If the hue you like is dark, try one that's a shade or two lighter on the color card instead. Conversely, if you're considering neutrals, particularly for a large room, test a hue that's one or two shades stronger than the one you really like. Neutrals tend to become too bland in large spaces. Keep in mind your walls' texture too. Rough surfaces, such as stucco or brick, do not reflect as much light as smooth walls, so they'll look darker than smooth walls painted the same color.

OPPOSITE: Light tan walls provide a neutral backdrop that blends with the sofa. **CENTER:** Spicy red is more dramatic, showing off the sofa and blending with the draperies. The uniform envelope of color is cozy and welcoming. **BELOW:** A darker tan creates a quiet, unfussy look that's richer than the light tan. There's more emphasis on the windows now, because of the contrast between the draperies and the walls.

Any fabric in any room can be the starting point for a color scheme. In the bedroom and bath, use your bedding and drapery fabrics for inspiration. In fact, using coordinated fabrics in two adjoining rooms offers an easy way to create a visual connection while giving each space its own color personality. A plaid and two florals in the same colorway unify this bedroom and bath. (A colorway is a color or combination of colors that runs through a collection of fabrics, making them easy to mix and match.) In the bedroom *opposite*, the background yellow from the floral was chosen for the walls, creating an airy, spacious feeling. In the bathroom *above*, red covers the walls. The vibrant color makes the room feel nurturing and inviting; white woodwork, cabinetry, and tile floor balance the red. The vaulted ceiling over the tub area is also white, balancing the expanse of the tub. The mirror reflects and doubles the red color, enhancing the feeling of enfolding warmth.

ABOVE AND RIGHT: The curtain fabric suggested red for the walls in the bathroom. A coordinating floral in the bedroom inspired yellow for that space. OPPOSITE: When combining florals, plaids, checks, and stripes, let one color dominate; a second and third in smaller amounts enliven the mix.

Here's the lesson from the photos on pages 102–107 stated another way: If you fall in love with a fabric, think about the mood you want the room to have and then let the fabric guide you. For this bedroom (decorated for a fund-raising showhouse), the goal was to create a soothing, comforting environment. To interior designer Amy Cornell Hammond, green offers the quickest path to that goal, evoking a quiet, gardenlike retreat. Because the room receives a lot of light, she felt it could take darker walls without feeling gloomy. Accordingly, she chose the green from the tulip fabric and applied it to the walls, using a variety of shades in a dragged and striated paint technique. Green plaid for the bed skirt and canopy and green upholstery on a chair reinforce the color theme, while raspberry fabrics pull out the red in the floral and add life to the scheme. Plenty of white keeps the room airy and fresh. Note that you can pull out the fabric's third color in tiny doses for an accent. A pair of decorative bed pillows, *opposite*, brings out the blue in the fabric and the rug. Red and green remain dominant, however, so the scheme has a clear personality.

LEFT AND OPPOSITE: The best color for the walls isn't necessarily the dominant one in your fabric. This tulip fabric is mostly white, but the print would lose its impact in a white room. Red, green, or yellow walls offer more interest.

WHAT COLOR FOR A DARK ROOM? If your room receives little natural light, your first thought might be to paint it white to lighten it or yellow to simulate sunshine. But remember that you'll be relying primarily on artificial light when you're using the room; choose a color that looks good under the kind of lighting you have, whether it's incandescent, halogen, or fluorescent. Because incandescent light is yellow, it can actually make pale yellow walls look washed out, while lavender tones will appear muddy. Terra-cotta, peach, and apricot, however, will look warm and welcoming. Under warm or daylight-balanced fluorescent light, colors will appear clearer, possibly even cold. Under halogen light, colors will look intense, but lighting an entire room with halogen lights may not be practical.

If you choose the darkest accent color or most intense tone in a fabric, you can create unexpected drama in a small space, such as a powder room *(right)*. Look for a wallpaper or paint that's as dark as or even a little darker than the note in the fabric. For visual relief, keep the ceiling and trim white.

OPTION 2 CHOOSE A COLOR YOU LOVE.

What if your primary fabric is a solid color? Suddenly you're faced with too many choices. To narrow the field, refer to the color wheel for ideas about which colors will harmonize with your solid. Think about how those colors make you feel. Are you comfortable with intense color on the walls or do you prefer softer, lighter, or more muted shades? After you narrow your choices, apply test swatches to the walls or to pieces of poster board to see how the colors work with your furnishings.

Denim blue upholstery with red piping, for example, might suggest yellow, red, coral, or periwinkle for the walls. Yellow would be warm, red or coral would be vibrant, and periwinkle would be calming. The yellow-green *opposite* is a less predictable choice for the walls, but here's why it works: Yellow-green occupies the same side of the color wheel as blue but, because of the yellow element, the color is warm and lively. The yellow-green is also the same intensity as the denim. Lighter values of this same pairing—soft celery green and silver-blue—team up effectively too (see pages 92–93).

ABOVE: The darkest tone in the fabric at the window led to the choice of coordinating wallpaper that turns this room into a glowing little space. OPPOSITE: Pairing yellow-green walls with denim blue upholstery creates a stylish, contemporary look.

CARING FOR DECORATIVE FABRICS To keep your drapery and upholstery fabrics looking fresh and the colors vibrant, carefully vacuum or brush regularly to remove dust and pet hair. Secure loose buttons, trim, or threads before vacuuming so you don't clog the vacuum cleaner. You can also tumble curtains and bedding in the dryer to shake out the dust. In case of spills on sofas and chairs, blot quickly—don't rub—with white paper towels or white towels. (Colored towels may fade onto the fabric you're cleaning.) If a stain remains, use a commercial spot cleaner recommended for upholstery fabrics, or try a homemade solution of 1 teaspoon of liquid dish detergent, ¼ teaspoon of white vinegar, and 1 quart of warm water. Test first in an inconspicuous spot. Apply the solution and let it sit 10 minutes; then rinse and blot dry.

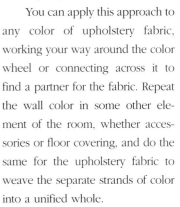

Starting with a solid-color fabric yields a more evolved, less matched look. It also gives you more freedom to choose a color you love. Interior designer Laura Miller found a buttery yellow that provided a cheerful backdrop for her red love seat, slipcovered sofa, and toile chair. Other choices that would work with her upholstery include leaf green, which would create more contrast and more drama; raspberry, which would turn up the heat for a monochromatic scheme with lots of energy; and gray, which would be formal and sedate.

At the other end of her living room, sage green and white combine with the same yellow for a quieter, subtler harmony. Yellow and green are neighbors on the color wheel, so they make natural partners. Here, dark wood and black accessories provide the deepest notes that punctuate the combination, and a collection of majolica repeats the green and yellow theme. The green could also be paired with peach, terra-cotta, or rose for more contrast; for a more subdued look, a deeper green would work.

You can apply this approach to any color of upholstery fabric, working your way around the color wheel or connecting across it to find a partner for the fabric. Repeat the wall color in some other element of the room, whether accessories or floor covering, and do the same for the upholstery fabric to weave the separate strands of color into a unified whole.

OPPOSITE: Red and yellow make a happy, eye-catching combination, cooled with accents of green and expanses of white. LEFT: Inspiration for color schemes can come from collections as well as fabrics. Yellow and green majolica translates into a lighter shade of yellow for the walls and soft green for love seat upholstery.

COLOR CONCEPTS
LIGHT AND COLOR

Color is light, and the color you perceive an object to have will change with the amount and type of light falling on the object. The artificial light you rely on in your home is most likely to be incandescent. This light is yellowish and warm, although a new type of bulb corrects the yellow so colors appear truer and clearer (see page 165 for more information). Halogen bulbs produce crisp white light that makes colors look more intense. But halogen bulbs are expensive compared to other types, and they must be used and handled with care. When you install the bulbs, wear disposable plastic gloves—the oils in your skin can cut the bulb's life in half. Because halogen bulbs generate so much heat, you must keep the bulbs a safe distance from the ceiling, walls, and table-top displays so surfaces and objects don't get scorched. Fluorescent light is typically bright and clear. Buy warm bulbs or daylight-balanced bulbs rather than cool-light bulbs, which give a sickly greenish cast.

B

C

A

Natural light varies with the time of day, the weather, and your geographic location. (The light in the Southwest really is different from that in Maine or the Midwest.) To test the effect of natural light on the colors you plan to use, buy a quart of each and paint samples on poster board to move around the room. If your house is surrounded by trees, the light that enters will have a greenish cast, which can change certain shades of yellow to an unhealthy yellow-green in high summer. Other colors may not be as affected by the filtering effect, and your eye (and your expectations) will compensate to some extent for any changes.

A At midday, the red walls have a rosy cast; by lamplight, the red appears distinctly warmer. **B** Without direct sunlight, the green walls appear cooler and bluer; with morning sun, the color is brighter and lighter. **C** Indirect light at midday emphasizes the neutral wall color; by late afternoon, the light is more orange and warms the room color. **D** Incandescent light, the most common indoor lighting, casts a yellowish glow that makes the red wall appear warmer in tone.

D

Whether your furnishings are Mission-style oak, country pine, or high-style mahogany, the beauty of the wood deserves a background that shows it to best advantage. The question, however, is not really what color goes with oak or mahogany, but rather, what color will best enhance your wood's finish. Each type of wood has a characteristic color and grain pattern, and the color also can be altered with stain. Furniture makers have used stains and varnishes for centuries, both to enhance the appearance of the grain and to change the color of the wood. The stains sold at home improvement centers are generally named for the types of wood they simulate: Maple, cherry, walnut, mahogany, ebony, oak, and fruitwood are the most common types.

Over time, wood furnishings acquire a rich patina that gives the sur-

QUESTION 7
WHAT COLOR WILL LOOK BEST WITH MY WOOD FURNITURE?

face depth and complexity. Newer woods and veneers may lack this complexity, but they still have an overall color tone that may be yellow, orange, red-brown, bluish brown, or dark brown. To choose wall colors or fabrics that will enhance your wood pieces, consider the dominant hues in the finish. Also consider whether you prefer the drama of high contrast or the richness of low-contrast pairings. Against light walls (such as yellow, mushroom gray, or sage), dark and reddish woods stand out boldly, calling attention to themselves. Against dark walls (such as navy and forest), dark woods blend in, while blond or light woods pop dramatically. Don't worry about all the wood pieces in a room matching—the casual, comfortable, gathered-over-time look of mixed woods is perfectly appropriate today.

Deep red walls match the warm tones of
the wainscoting to create a unified color
effect in the breakfast nook. The yellow
finish on the chairs and the worn,
unpainted tabletop brighten the corner.

Q. WHAT COLOR WILL LOOK BEST WITH MY WOOD FURNITURE?

OPTION 1 CHOOSE HIGH CONTRAST FOR EMPHASIS.

Dark finishes, such as mahogany, walnut, or cherry, stand out in sharp relief against any light color, whether it's a tint of green or blue or a hue from the sunny side of the color wheel. In the same way, light wood shows up boldly against dark or strong color on the walls. The contrast calls more attention to the furniture, a plus if you have a fine piece you want to focus on. If you have a lot of dark furniture in a light-color room, however, the space may feel busier than it would if the furniture blended in. If you love the look of dark wood against light walls (or light furniture against dark walls), keep furniture arrangements orderly and streamlined to offset the impression of crowding. To achieve high contrast with medium-tone finishes, keep the wall color soft and light, creating as much difference as possible between the values of the wood color and the wall.

ABOVE: Interior designer Laura Miller tries not to match things too closely—she prefers a more natural, evolved look. For her bedroom, she chose a wall color that's cream with a touch of green for a mellow, peaceful feeling. The bed is dressed in cream and white. The pale walls focus attention on the mahogany bed and other furnishings. Orderly, symmetrical arrangements of a few well-chosen accessories maintain the aura of tranquillity. OPPOSITE: Stacked wicker suitcases lead the eye from the top of the dresser to the framed bird print. Seashells on each side complete the arrangement. Mahogany usually suggests formality, so pairing it with wicker suitcases and seashells surprises with a fresh effect.

You can also use the colors in the furniture finish as a cue for wall colors. If the dominant color in the wood appears to be red, then a green background will enhance and intensify the wood's hue. Golden-yellow woods look handsome against warm red as well as earthy greens, teal, or eggplant. Brown woods with yellow undertones relate to buttery walls yet stand out boldly for high-contrast drama. Antique woods, which have a patina that offers depth and complexity, may combine several tones—that's why they can look good against a variety of light or dark colors.

OPPOSITE: Apple green walls complement wood furnishings that have a definite red cast in their finish. BELOW: The yellow finish on a country French chair glows like sunshine against rosy walls. A similar hue in the picture frame underscores the effect. RIGHT: You can combine wood pieces of different periods and colors, but keep the pieces in a similar tonal range for greater harmony.

OPTION 2 CHOOSE LOW CONTRAST FOR A RICH, SUBTLE LOOK.

Pairing hues of equal intensity or value creates low contrast. This doesn't mean the furniture fades into the background, however. When you put a dark mahogany chest or ebony table against a deep red or blue-green wall *(right and below)*, you create a dynamic balance between two hues of equal strength. The value of the wood color equals that of the wall. The same principle works with medium brown woods and muted or medium-tone colors *(below left)*; the effect is more restrained because the tones are subdued. Warm neutrals, such as taupe, mushroom, or khaki, bring out the rich, toasty notes in medium brown woods. The furniture shows up handsomely, but the effect is quiet and low-key, producing a different kind of drama from that created by high contrast.

OPPOSITE: Gray walls provide a subtle backdrop for the honeyed tones of a country French armoire. TOP RIGHT: Give a room a color boost with complementary accents. Bright green Osage oranges pop against red walls. BOTTOM LEFT: The minimal color contrast between medium brown wood and a neutral-color wall evokes calm. BOTTOM RIGHT: A nearly black finish on a three-legged table snaps to attention in front of a blue-green wall.

CARING FOR WOOD FURNITURE To protect the finish on your wood furniture, dust often, using a lamb's-wool duster or a very slightly dampened cloth. Either of these will keep the dust from simply flying around and resettling on the furniture. Avoid using spray polishes that contain silicone or synthetic materials. Over time these will build up a hazy film. Instead, apply paste wax once every year or two, buffing with a soft cloth or lamb's-wool pad to achieve a deep shine. Use a paste wax formulated for furniture; high-quality waxes contain beeswax or a mixture of beeswax and carnauba wax.

COLOR AND WOOD

Color preferences are entirely personal, but when you're choos-ing background colors for furniture, you may find that some do a better job than others of bringing out the natural beauty of wood. These six backgrounds for a honey-toned pine cupboard and frame illustrate the impact of color on wood.

The warmth of the wood shows up well against a medium green (A). This green brings out the yellow tones in the wood and balances them with cool contrast. A clear minty green (B) could seem a little gaudy, but a pale gray-green (C) is an attractive, low-key choice. Intense, bright blue (D) brings out the wood's orange tones, but you have to love high contrast to live with this much bold color; the contrast could seem harsh. Terracotta or pale orange (E) draws out the orange in the wood but is so similar in tone that the wood is nearly lost. Yellow (F) brings out the wood's orange and yellow tones and emphasizes an overall warmth, but like E, it doesn't enhance the wood.

C

D

A

B

E

F

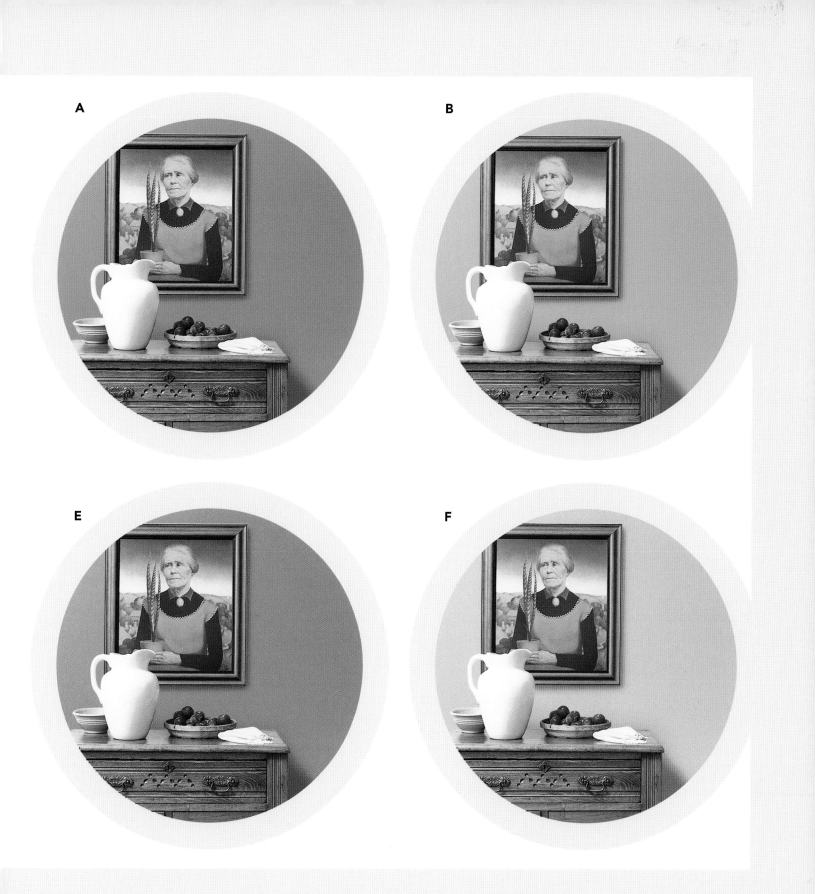

Cabinets dominate the walls in a kitchen, so if they're a dark cherry or Mediterranean finish (popular in the 1970s), they make the whole kitchen feel dark. In the bathroom, tiled walls install color permanently and limit your decorating options. Short of replacing kitchen cabinets and tearing out tiles and fixtures, how can you give these rooms a facelift?

In the kitchen, you have a couple of options. Refacing the cabinetry, with either laminate or wood veneer, is less expensive than putting in new cabinets—but cutting and gluing the laminate in place is hard work and requires skill. Painting cabinets is an achievable do-it-yourself project if you're patient and willing to prepare surfaces carefully. You can even paint old laminate cabinets using a primer especially for-

QUESTION 8

HOW CAN I UPDATE MY KITCHEN AND BATH?

mulated for glossy surfaces. This type of primer eliminates the need for sanding or deglossing and can be used under latex or oil paint. If you like your wood cabinets but wish they had a different finish, you can strip and refinish them, if the veneer is in good condition.

To update a bathroom, choose a wall color that works with the tiles but takes the color scheme in a fresher direction. To increase the impact of the new color, apply the same color to cabinetry, and use rugs, towels, curtains, and shower curtains to underscore the new look. If you have truly awful tiles and fixtures, don't despair—you can have them reglazed for a fraction of what it would cost to tear them out and replace them.

Painting cabinets and walls transforms the appearance of a kitchen. Dark brown cabinets and bright blue tiles (see page 128) gave way to creamy white and mushroom gray for a fresh, serene look.

Q. HOW CAN I UPDATE MY KITCHEN AND BATH?

OPTION 1 PAINT THE CABINETRY AND TILES.

If the cabinetry is solidly built and in good condition and your kitchen layout works well for you, consider painting the cabinets to change the color and mood of the room. Interior designer Laura Miller was faced with a double challenge in her home's kitchen: Dark brown cabinets lined the walls and island (*below*), while bright blue tile went from countertop to ceiling. But the cabinets and solid-surface countertops were in good condition, the kitchen floor plan was comfortable, and the vintage character of the space appealing, so Laura decided to paint rather than embark on a complete overhaul.

WHEN TO HIRE PROFESSIONALS Tile requires special preparation to be painted, so it's not really a do-it-yourself job. Miller hired painters who specialize in spray applications. They removed the cabinet doors, then cleaned and sanded the cabinets and roughened the tiles before spraying these surfaces with an oil-base enamel paint. The doors were painted separately. Miller doesn't cook much, so the tile isn't subjected to heavy scrubbing; in a kitchen that is heavily used, a better choice might be to have the tiles reglazed (see page 132). Sprayed surfaces can be more difficult to touch up when they get nicked, because the application leaves a slightly rough texture; patting on paint with a sponge works for small fix-ups.

Miller used the same creamy color for cabinetry, woodwork, and tile that she used for trim throughout the house. On the soffit above the cabinets and on the stair wall, she replaced wallpaper with a mushroom-color paint that sets off her collection of brown transferware. New hardwood flooring complements

BEFORE

RIGHT: Bright blue tile from countertop to ceiling and blue foil wallpaper on the soffit contrasted sharply with dark wood cabinets. The kitchen felt gloomy and oppressive.
OPPOSITE: Cream color paint brought new serenity to the room. Stainless steel door panels on the refrigerator and dishwasher and stainless steel miniblinds in the window add clean, contemporary style.

For continuity, the Millers' kitchen wall and trim colors continue up the stairwell to the second floor. OPPOSITE ABOVE AND BELOW: Here's another way to deal with dark cabinets and blue tile. Painting cabinets white and walls green updates the look and integrates the blue tile backsplash into a more harmonious color scheme. Stencils on the soffit repeat the blue and add accents of color.

the vintage look of the cabinetry, and stainless steel doors on the refrigerator and dishwasher introduce light-reflecting surfaces that enhance the brighter look of the room.

WHEN TO DO IT YOURSELF To update dark cabinetry and incorporate tile backsplashes like those *below right* into a fresher color scheme, paint the cabinets and walls yourself. Remove all doors, drawers, and hardware. Clean all surfaces with a grease-cutting cleaning solution and dry them thoroughly. Fill any dents or deep scratches with wood dough. If you plan to change the hardware, choose it first and check to see whether you'll need to drill new holes. If so, fill the old holes with wood dough.

Prime the cabinetry before painting. If you're using an ordinary latex primer, roughen surfaces with medium-grade sandpaper to help the paint adhere better. Or use a specially formulated primer for glossy surfaces. Depending on the brand, the primer may be labeled a primer-sealer stainkiller, latex enamel undercoater primer sealer, or glossy surface primer. Check the label to make sure the primer is formulated for use on laminate and glossy wood; the label should also state that no sanding or deglossing is required.

Apply at least two coats of paint, using a heavy-duty gloss or semigloss enamel (either oil-base or latex). Roll the paint onto large, flat areas, but for paneling and tight spots, use a brush—natural bristle for oil-base paint, synthetic bristle for latex. Set drawers on end and raise cabinet doors on bricks or blocks so you can paint the edges.

BEFORE

A NEW VIEW Replacing cabinet doors with glass brings a more open feeling to your kitchen, adding a sense of depth to the walls by allowing you see into the cabinets. Remove the center panel of the door (you may have to trim it out with a saw) and have glass cut to fit the opening. Cut ¼×¼-inch molding to frame the opening, mitering the corners. Paint the molding to match the cabinet door. Lay the glass in the opening and hold it in place with the molding strips, securing them with wood glue and brads.

REGLAZING PORCELAIN AND TILE

In the bathroom, one generation's idea of stylish tile and tub colors is the next generation's nightmare. One option is to have ceramic tile and porcelain tubs and sinks resurfaced or reglazed. Reglazing a bathtub costs about $350 to $400. To find a professional tile-and-tub refinisher, look in the Yellow Pages under "Bathtubs and Sinks—Repair and Refinish." Look for a refinisher who uses an acrylic or silica-based polymer product. (Avoid urethane-based finishes, which contain carcinogenic chemicals.) Request references, and ask homeowners how long ago they had the job done and how well the new surfaces have held up.

The procedure includes applying a chemical bonding agent, a primer, and a top coat, using high-volume low-pressure spray equipment. Most companies also offer the option of applying a nonslip surface to the bottom of the tub along with the new finish. Depending on the process, the finish may take from a few hours up to 48 hours to cure. Reglazed surfaces should only be cleaned with nonabrasive cleaners. Although colors are available, remember that the grout will be painted the same color as the tile. White or off-white will give you the most versatility.

BEFORE

KEEPING CLEAN Tile, marble, and porcelain may look like they're indestructible, but cleaning them with abrasive powders will damage them. To remove soap scum from porcelain tubs and ceramic tile, use a nonabrasive bathroom cleaner, a tub-and-tile spray, or a solution of white vinegar and water. To clean mildew from grout, use a solution of ¾ cup bleach to 1 gallon of water and scrub with a toothbrush. Clean marble with soap and water and rinse well.

OPPOSITE BOTTOM: Pink ceramic tile and a tub in a different shade of pink pose a decorating challenge. In preparation for refinishing, green paper protects walls, baseboard, and fixtures from the reglazing material, which is sprayed on. **OPPOSITE TOP AND ABOVE:** Now the tile and tub are gleaming white, with the original black tile molding capping the wall tile. The bathroom's original marble sink was reinstalled and skirted to hide the plumbing. Moiré wallpaper above the tile wall shows off green English transferware plates.

OPTION 2 CHANGE THE WALLS TO SUIT THE TILE.

Painting tile and cabinetry is less expensive than tearing them out and replacing them, but it's still an investment of time and trouble. If you don't mind the color of your tile or cabinets, use them to guide your choice of wall color. Then add fabric, art, rugs, or accessories to build the new scheme. The green-tiled bathroom *below* illustrates two options. For a crisp, clean look, paint the woodwork, walls, and ceiling white, in keeping with the fixtures. For more color impact, choose a wallpaper that harmonizes with the tile and use rugs, shower curtain, and towels to introduce additional color accents.

The ubiquitous 1950s-pink is among the most challenging of tile colors because it was made in a variety of shades and combined with

ABOVE LEFT: Pairing light green tiles with white enlarges the sense of space, and a geometric stencil design keeps the wall from seeming bland. **ABOVE RIGHT:** If you opt for a wallcovering, consider one that's a shade lighter than the tile. This mimics the effect of atmospheric perspective, in which colors become paler or more muted with distance—you'll create the illusion of loftier space. **OPPOSITE:** This bathroom suffered from too much of a good thing, with 1950s-pink tile on walls, floor, and vanity. As an antidote to excess, a pale gray was applied to the walls above the tile and a slightly darker hue to the vanity cabinet. White towels and accessories further lighten the look. Another option: A minty green would draw out the peach tones in the pink tile.

BEFORE

The Real Thing Cabinets may be made of particleboard, medium-density fiberboard (MDF), or plywood. Because all three are composed of wood products, cabinets manufactured from them are considered solid wood. The cabinet boxes, doors, and drawers may be faced with wood veneer or with laminate, which is made in a wide variety of textures and colors, including various simulated wood grains. Generally you can feel the difference: Wood veneer retains some of the roughness of wood grain, while laminate does not.

BEFORE

black, mint green, pale blue, or burgundy. If you like the shade of pink, build on it by painting walls and cabinetry the same color or slightly lighter. To tone it down, look for a wallpaper that incorporates the tile color; the pattern will help distract the eye from the tile. Or paint the wall above the tile in a warm neutral that blends with the tile but calms its impact.

If you have neutral tiles, you're in luck. With a coat of paint or a roll of wallpaper, you can shift the room's color personality from cool to warm or vice versa. Dusty pink accent tiles and almond-color paint bring out the pink tones in the pickled cabinetry, *above*. When pale yellow is applied to the walls, *opposite*, the cabinetry's warmer notes emerge, and the dusty pink accents recede in importance.

Cabinets that are bleached, pickled, or even a light natural wood finish can also be treated like neutrals. If, on the other hand, you've inherited the dark cherry or deep brown cabinets that were popular in the 1970s, play up the warmth with deep color on the walls and floor—earthy, toasty hues such as brick red, cinnamon, ocher, or pumpkin will harmonize with the wood stain, and if you add little accent lamps and brass accessories to catch and reflect light, the effect will be rich, cozy, and elegant. Don't try to lighten a kitchen filled with dark cabinets by painting the walls a light color; the high contrast will only focus attention on the cabinets. If you want to lighten and brighten, paint the cabinets too (see pages 128–131).

OPPOSITE: All of the colors in a room affect each other and the way you perceive them. Almond-color walls brought out the pink tones in the bleached oak cabinets and off-white wall tiles. BELOW: Now a very pale yellow on the walls emphasizes the warmer tones and connects the room visually to the dining room beyond.

Brick is the material of choice for houses if you want low maintenance and fire resistance, but it's usually confined to the exterior and, inside, to fireplaces. In fact, because it withstands the heat of a fire, brick is the most common choice for lining fireboxes and facing fireplace surrounds. Depending on the style of your home, the fireplace surround may be a few discreet rows of bricks or a commanding structure. Beyond the fireplace, if you have a contemporary-style house or if you've added a room, tackled a loft conversion, or remodeled, you may have an expanse of interior brick to deal with. Whether it broods darkly over your room or brings comfortable rustic character depends largely on the color of the brick and how well it works with your room's color scheme. The clay that goes into making the brick determines the color of the

QUESTION 9

HOW DO I WORK WITH THE COLOR OF MY BRICK?

final product. Different mineral compositions respond to firing differently, yielding hues ranging from buff and yellow to salmon pink to dark red-brown. If coatings such as sand or limestone are added during firing, they will affect the color and texture as well. To integrate a brick feature into your decorating scheme, first decide whether you want to focus attention on the feature or downplay its presence in the room. Use its hue to choose wall colors accordingly. If the brick is a color you cannot live with, consider painting it. In the case of a fireplace, match the brick to the room's woodwork to emphasize its role as a natural focal point. Or paint the brick to blend with the walls and match the mantel to the room's trim. Choose a satin or semigloss paint for easy cleaning (if soot from the fireplace is a problem, for example).

The medium red-brown color of brick functions as a neutral; it can go with anything. Sage green complements the red, while sunny yellow enhances the warmth of the brick.

Q. **HOW DO I WORK WITH THE COLOR OF MY BRICK?**

OPTION 1 LOOK FOR THE BRICK'S DOMINANT COLOR.

Treat the brick's color as you would a fabric, paint, or carpet color, and use the color wheel to guide you toward harmonious hues. Brick that's primarily pink, salmon, or light red works well with soft yellows, cool greens, and creamy antique whites. Yellow or buff-color brick combines handsomely with neutrals such as cool grays or warm browns; look for subdued or grayed shades to blend with the earth tones in the brick. The greater the contrast between the color of your brick and the color of adjacent walls, the more attention you'll draw to the brick. Incorporate touches of the brick color elsewhere in the room, in fabrics or accessories, to knit it into your design scheme.

OPPOSITE AND TOP: Remodeling brought an exterior brick wall indoors and inspired the addition of an arch with bricks laid to look as though they were original construction recently uncovered. Teamed with pale yellow walls and white trim, the salmon pink brick brings warmth and architectural character to the dining area. **ABOVE:** Off-white walls pick up the subdued tones of the brickwork, which was extended higher when this room's ceiling was raised. The lower wall was originally painted, and the homeowner painstakingly stripped the paint, then whitewashed old and new brick to blend them together.

Instead of trying to counteract the dominating effect of dark brick by painting the adjoining walls a lighter color (which would only contrast with and emphasize the brick), choose a neutral that's in the same tonal range as the brick. This integrates the brick into the room, creating a more harmonious, unified whole. In the dining room *opposite* and the adjoining morning room *below,* the brick is a brown-red, so a brownish taupe for the walls emphasizes the warm effect. A

cream color on the ceiling balances the dark wall color. The ceiling beams, which originally had a dark stain, were painted a shade darker than the walls to keep them from looming overhead. If the walls are the darkest element in a room, the space can feel oppressive; to prevent this, include a darker element. Here, black upholstery on the dining chairs and a black lacquered chest make the walls seem lighter by comparison, so the room feels rich with character and atmosphere.

In the morning room, the walls were washed and ragged with layers of color inspired by a painting in the dining room *opposite.* A muted taupe-brown that harmonizes with the brown tones in the brick outlines the ceiling in the morning room and warms the entry hall and dining area.

OPTION 2 **PAINT THE BRICK.**

If the natural color of the brick doesn't suit your decorating style, consider painting it. To downplay its presence, paint it to match the walls. To play up the architectural importance of the feature, paint it to match the trim in the room. If that draws too much attention to the element, color the brick a shade or two darker or lighter than the walls and paint the mantel to match the trim.

To paint raw brick, first apply a good-quality exterior latex primer, which adheres to brick better than interior primers do. Alternatively, you can use a primer-sealer stainkiller. On previously painted brick, prime with a stain-blocking primer-sealer formulated for glossy surfaces (a deglossing primer) so you won't have to sand first. Brush on the primer, working it into all the crevices. Then apply two coats of the desired color of latex paint (oil-base or alkyd paints are not recommended for brick, because they trap moisture). High gloss or semigloss will show off the texture of the brick better than a flat finish and will be easier to clean.

OPPOSITE AND TOP RIGHT: Painting the brick fireplace to match the walls retains the texture while eliminating a difficult-to-live-with color of brick. BOTTOM RIGHT: If you're repainting brick, prime with a deglossing primer first to help the paint adhere. To focus attention on the fireplace, paint the brick surround darker than the walls, but match the mantel to the woodwork to tie it to the rest of the room.

PAINT IN HASTE; REPENT AT LEISURE Think carefully before committing to painting brick—removing the paint later is a slow, painstaking, and labor-intensive job. A faster (and more expensive) alternative is to hire professionals to sandblast off the paint, but this risks damaging the surface of the brick as well as the mortar joints. If you decide to tackle paint removal yourself, use sandpaper and a wire brush. To remove fresh paint accidentally splashed onto brick, use a commercial paint remover or a solution of trisodium phosphate (TSP) and water. (TSP is available at home improvement centers.) Let the solvent soften the paint; then brush with a stiff-bristle brush and rinse with clear water. For more on cleaning brick, visit the website of the Brick Industry Association at www.bia.org.

COLOR CONCEPTS
COLOR SCHEMES

Whether you're starting from scratch or updating a room, devel-oping a new color scheme can seem intimidating and overwhelming. Starting with a fabric you love is one good way to narrow your choices. Another is to start with an object whose colors inspire you, such as a piece of artwork, a porcelain bowl, or an Oriental rug. Use those colors to create the palette for walls, floor, furnishings, and accessories.

For example, interior designer Roberta Ketchin found inspiration in the painting *opposite* and translated it into a multicolor palette for the home shown on pages 17–21. She didn't try to match the painting color for color, but rather used it as a starting point for selecting bright hues that would work well together throughout the house.

The red, yellow, and green in the painting show up as a rosy wine shade in the dining room, a palmetto green for the kitchen, and a complex yellow for the living room, entry, and stair landing. Upholstery fabrics play on the theme with solids, plaids, and prints in a range of greens, yellows, and reds. Rugs, pillows, and accessories, such as painted furniture, porcelain bowls, and flowers, reinforce the color scheme. In each room, a different color dominates, imbuing each space with a distinct personality. The repetition of colors throughout the house knits rooms together and creates a feeling of comfortable cohesion.

How do you decide which colors to put where? Start with the rooms where you and your family spend the most time. What mood do you want to create? (See pages 68–69 for how colors can affect the way you feel in a room.) Which of the colors in your "object of inspiration" will help you achieve that mood? Use that color for the walls and perhaps a tint of a secondary color for the ceiling and floor. For furnishings and window treatments, look for fabrics that combine your inspiration-piece colors in varying amounts and shades. Solid-color fabrics will have the greatest impact; prints or plaids add interest and variety.

A landscape painting inspires, rather than dictates, color choices for walls, upholstery, and accessories. The claret red on the dining room walls, *left,* is cooler than the bold red in the art, while the grass green kitchen, *right,* closely resembles the green in the springtime landscape.

Solid color upholstery, *left,* creates the most color impact in a room, while plaids and figured patterns, *right,* help add interesting variety. Pillows, rugs, and even a painted chair repeat the key colors of red, yellow, and green in varying shades and tones, helping tie adjacent spaces together.

White walls—you either love 'em or hate 'em. Perhaps you go with white by default; choosing a color seems risky, with too many options, and you don't know whether you'll like it until the job is done. Or maybe you like bold colors and your partner doesn't, so you settle for white. Because it goes with anything, white has come to be seen as the safe choice for houses going on the market and for apartments. It's that unimaginative overuse of white that has led to the color's reputation as boring and sterile. But it doesn't have to be that way. White brings in the light; it's airy, clean, serene, and contemplative. It's the perfect backdrop for bold artwork and contemporary furniture. (That's why the walls are always white in contemporary art museums.) And white has more personality than you think. Paint companies offer collections of whites that range in tone from coffee-with-cream to mint,

QUESTION 10

I LIKE WHITE, BUT HOW CAN I MAKE IT INTERESTING?

pink, and violet. The paint chips by themselves appear to be pastels or various shades of beige (except for a few pure whites), but when you get them on the wall, the overall effect is white—with an undertone that's either cool or warm. These shades mean that you can enjoy the light-reflecting, space-expanding qualities of white without succumbing to tedium. As with any color, painting or staining the doors, door frames, window frames, and any other trim a contrasting color can enhance the white on the walls, bringing out the undertones. Bright white trim will make beige-white walls appear slightly darker by contrast, while cool whites will appear clear and fresh when outlined with bright white. Be cautious about pairing bright white with antique or creamy white, because the latter may look dirty by contrast. Test poster-size swatches before committing to paint on the walls.

To make the most of brilliant white, use it in rooms with abundant natural light. An all-white scheme in an oddly shaped room minimizes the choppy architecture and enlarges the sense of space. Touches of color in plants or accessories provide just enough contrast to bring the room to life. Otherwise you might feel as though you're looking for polar bears in a blizzard.

OPTION 1 LAYER WHITE ON WHITE AND ADD TEXTURE.

White-on-white decorating creates a pristine purity conducive to contemplation and relaxation. With all surfaces and details bathed in the same light-reflecting brilliance, your eye focuses on shape and texture, and ordinary objects take on sculptural beauty. Textures supply the variety needed to keep things interesting: Shiny damask, smooth porcelain, chalky plaster, fuzzy chenille, matte cotton, and weathered painted wood will reflect light differently, providing the contrast that the eye craves and engaging the sense of touch as well.

Also incorporate different shades of white. In paints and fabrics, most whites are either warm (leaning toward yellow, rose, or beige tones) or cool (with a hint of gray or icy blue). Off-white, antique

white, ivory, ecru, and cream evoke romantic warmth but remain within the family of white. Grayed whites can look dirty next to brilliant whites, and some decorators shy away from using pure white altogether, because it makes other shades appear muddy.

Of course, no room in the real world is totally white. Houseplants, fireplaces, artwork, and accessories introduce touches of color that keep white rooms from feeling sterile and clinical. The contrast only enhances the beauty of white on white.

OPPOSITE: Contrasting color in the architecture, furnishings, and accessories keeps an all-white room from feeling chilly or sterile. CENTER: Slipcovers smooth out the envelope of white, giving the chairs a solid shape that has more visual weight than do leggy chairs. BELOW: A white background shows off the sculptural quality of furnishings and flea market finds.

OPTION 2 WARM UP WHITE WITH NEUTRALS.

A white room filled with white furnishings is too much of a good thing, but if you add natural textures and a rich array of neutral colors, white becomes the clean, serene backdrop for comfort and relaxation. White sets the stage for a sleek contemporary look, but it's also the key to modern country style. To achieve that livable quality, include the full range of wood tones, from blond to cherry to ebony, when you select tables, picture frames, and accessories. Leave golden pine floors bare, or add sisal or jute area rugs for extra texture. Use wicker baskets for storage and select weathered wood or rusted metal accessories to introduce still more types of surfaces.

IS WHITE PRACTICAL? If you love white but think it's not for you because you have a houseful of kids and pets, don't be too quick to dismiss it. Walls painted with satin- or eggshell-finish latex can be wiped to remove jelly handprints. Washable cotton slipcovers on the sofa and chairs will make a major impact on the room's appearance and offer easy maintenance. Instead of sisal or jute area rugs, which will probably be too rough for little knees and feet, use a medium-tone or dark neutral rug to anchor seating pieces and to hide dirt and paw prints.

To maintain a mostly white envelope, add these touches sparingly. For a stronger color impact, bring in more neutrals. In addition to the expected browns, beiges, grays, and black, neutrals can include olive, ocher, blue-gray, and muted gray-green—colors readily found in nature. As with any color scheme, use a range of tones from dark to medium to light so the results will feel balanced and well-rounded.

LEFT: Glass, stone, sisal, wood, and wicker warm up a white room. Pale green and yellow can function like neutrals in a space like this. Soft sage green echoes the color of river rocks in a wooden dough bowl and the color of a folk art fish; a yellow wool blanket brings the color of sisal to the arm of the sofa. Subtlety, rather than bold contrast, is the key to achieving this look.

OPPOSITE: Open shelving is both functional and decorative when you can arrange serving pieces and collectibles in a tidy, orderly fashion. Olive-color mugs and orange ceramic flowerpots introduce earth tones that keep the kitchen from seeming stark. One dark element, the painting of pears, provides focus. BELOW RIGHT: Gray granite countertops anchor the expanse of white ceramic tile and painted cabinetry. In a sea of one color, a note of contrast provides the balance you need to feel comfortable. BELOW: Frosted glass shelves appear to float above the kitchen sink, enhancing the clean, serene atmosphere. Tile walls make hanging artwork tricky; clear monofilament suspends the carved wooden fish from the metal rods supporting the glass shelves.

An antique wardrobe, stripped of its paint, stores glassware, plates, and linens. Introducing a major furniture piece like this into an all-white room brings in character and color without disturbing the air of serenity that white-plus-neutrals evokes. Modern Dutch chairs offer warmer wood tones. If your table and chairs are mahogany and you long to lighten things up, cover the table with a floor-length cloth and sew simple slipcovers for the dining chairs. Even pinafore-style chair covers will make a difference.

Create a feeling of luxury with layers of white in different textures. Chenille, matelassé, and cotton can dress the bed for summer, while flannel and fleece in winter white bring snuggly comfort to the room. A painted cottage-style bedside table shows how subtle shades of green can serve as neutrals in no-color settings. If you find an antique bed you love but it's not quite a double-bed size, just let the full-size mattress overhang the frame slightly on each side. Once you dress the bed, no one will notice.

OPTION 3 ADD COLOR WITH FURNISHINGS AND ACCESSORIES.

White is a good choice if you like to redecorate often, introducing new window treatments, new bedding, and slipcovers to create a different color scheme. The shell of the room becomes a backdrop for the personality pieces you bring to it. This option may also appeal if you live in an apartment and don't want to invest the time and energy (not to mention the money) in painting the walls something other than white. Fabric, artwork, floor coverings, and accessories become the carriers of color. In the living room, chairs, sofas, and area rugs will have the most impact on the room's color mood, with pillows and accessories accenting the theme. In the bedroom, change the bedding and the area rug, and you change the look. Even in dining rooms, bathrooms, and kitchens, fabric introduces color—at the windows, on chair seats, in shower curtains and towels—and artwork and accessories reinforce it.

When you start with a white shell, your furnishings become the means of creating a color scheme. If you have one favorite color—say, orange—then using it on your sofa, a side chair, and perhaps a poster will stamp your room with personality. A touch of purple—on another side chair—provides the contrasting temperature (cool) and hue that make the orange pop. For even more zest, introduce another color or two. Magenta

OPPOSITE: Eye-popping color reminiscent of the 1960s jazzes up this loft space. When you're working with bright colors, limit yourself to two to four and let one hue dominate.

BUILDING A COLOR SCHEME Interior designer John Robert Wiltgen, who designed the room *opposite*, suggests limiting the number of colors you work with to two to four. That gives you enough for a pleasing variety without chaos. Let one color dominate in each room. In the living room, the sofa often wears the most important color, but a pair of chairs or a space-defining area rug could play the lead role instead. Repeat each color at least once elsewhere in a room; otherwise the lone color will stand out and look like a mistake. Use contrasting color to play up important architectural details, such as a handsome fireplace or interesting windows. White walls automatically make your furnishings and accessories the room's focal point. Emphasize them by choosing furnishings or objects with strong colors— or assign them a neutral dress code so they'll fade into the background.

is a step away from purple on the color wheel, and acid green is its complement; using small doses of each enlivens the scheme without detracting from the primary orange.

A white shell seems especially well-suited to bright, pure colors like those found in contemporary art and furnishings, but it's also a congenial foil for clear hues and ice cream colors. To keep the focus on an art collection, avoid fabrics with a lot of pattern. Instead, use solids in a range of values from light to dark. In the living room *below,* even the floor is white, with the herringbone floorboards pickled for a luminous effect. A triadic color scheme (three colors equally spaced on the color wheel) plays out in small doses of pink, blue, and yellow that skip around the space. Pink appears in three shades—pale on the chair, hot on the cushions on the Saarinen settee, and muted on the rug. Blue and yellow appear in three shades each as well. Holding three colors in nearly equal balance like this runs counter to the usual rule of allowing one color to dominate; this scheme succeeds because of the varying shades, the generous expanses of white, and the rug, which anchors the room's palette. The elements of black—in the paintings, piano, hearth, and rug—provide essential grounding, the darkest note that punctuates the light scheme.

With white as your unifying theme throughout the house, you can imbue each room with dramatically different colors in the fabrics and floor coverings and still have a sense of flow. Choose the brightest or boldest colors for the rooms where people gather to talk, eat, or play. For bedrooms or rooms where you want to relax and unwind, softer or more muted colors will promote rest. In a home office or study, consider which color promotes concentration for you. Turquoise and aqua are stimulating and energizing, for example, while purple is associated with inspiration. The good thing about starting with white is that it allows you to introduce strong color in small doses

that will delight your eye without overwhelming you. A cobalt blue cupboard, for example, adds zest to a calm white room. You'll want to repeat that color somewhere in the room, perhaps in a vase or painting, to anchor it. Otherwise, it will seem isolated and accidental.

OPPOSITE: Interior designer Julia Doyle keeps the furniture from competing with the art by restricting the fabric palette to solids and white. Bold color in this living room makes up for the lack of a view. The rug is based on a painting by artist Juan Gris. BELOW: Although Doyle doesn't match furniture to art or vice versa, the sofa pillows do relate to colors in a triptych by Robert Rauschenberg. Bringing the color down to the sofa complements the art and subtly enhances the sense of harmony and balance in the room.

RESOURCES

HOW DO I CONNECT ROOMS WITH COLOR?

Pages 7–15: Interior design, Amelia T. Handegan of amelia t. handegan, inc., 165-A King St., Charleston, SC 29401; 843/722-9373. Page 7: Paint custom-mixed. Ebonized spindle-back chairs, antique. Page 8: Antique incense burners on side table, black chinoiserie box, Queen Charlotte Antiques, Ltd., 173 King St., Charleston, SC 29401; fax 843/722-9037. Painting: Mickey Williams. Chinoiserie secretary, English, 1840. Page 9: Portrait, 18th-century French. Drapery fabric: Bergamo Fabrics (to the trade), 212/888-3333; fabric #13535, Savoy-Pumpkin. Pages 10–11: Paint custom-mixed. Tall French candlestick on sideboard, silver candlesticks on dining table, antique boxes throughout: Golden & Associates, Inc., 206 King St., Charleston, SC 29401; 843/723-8886. Antique silver container on sideboard, Croghan's Jewel Box, 308 King Street, Charleston, SC 29401. Entry, baseboards painted by Robert Shelton. Page 12: Paint, Benjamin Moore Bennington Gray. Center pillow on love seat, Piazza, 34-A Chalmers St., Charleston, SC 29401; 843/853-4555. Ticking on love seat, Schumacher. Page 14: Armchairs covered in Ultra Suede from Decorators Walk (to the trade). Stylist, Lynn McBride; photography, Cheryl Dalton.

Page 16: Interior design, David A. Herchik and Richard Looman, JDS Designs, Inc., 528 Eighth St. NE, Washington, DC 20002; 202/543-8631. Fabric on love seat and round skirted table, Cowtan & Tout/Larsen (to the trade). Fabric for window seat cushion: Chaine-Glant Textiles, Seattle, WA 98124; call for the name of a local store, 206/725-4444. Fabric for chair pad and antique stools: Vineleaf from Osborne & Little (to the trade). Fabric for antique lounge chairs: Bermuda Cloth, Scalamandre (to the trade). Flooring in kitchen: American Olean Tile. Wall color, garden room, similar to Sherwin Williams Madcap Violet SW1246; kitchen wall color similar to Sherwin Williams Pistachio SW 1429. Photography, Tom McWilliam; field editor, D.J. Carey.

Pages 17–21: Interior Design, Roberta Ketchin, Roberta Ketchin Interiors, Ali's Alley, 28 Hasell St., Charleston, SC 29401; 843/577-5770. Page 17: Sofa fabric: Greeff (available through decorators) #3050016, Colors I collection; sofa pillow fabrics: Wesley Hall, Inc. (Reva/Peridot, Clemintine/Ivory, Basket/Butter); skirted chair and fabric: Wesley Hall (Basket/Butter); French Regency chair and fabric: Wesley Hall, Inc. (Reva/Peridot). Chinoiserie side chair, handpainted and lacquered, Payne Street Imports. Pages 18–19: Entry and living room wallpaper: pattern #36000 from Harlequin in wallcovering book Casablanca; drapery fabric: Monkwell of Lee Jofa (#MF5492) in fabric book Bohemian Silks; chair fabric: Greeff (#3130087), Capri Collection; chairs, Sarreid Ltd. Pages 20–21: Wall paint: Duron (#7645D-Fairway); ceiling paint: Duron (#7734M-Cane); woodwork paint: Duron (#CW030W-Apple Peel); kitchen chair fabric: discontinued; kitchen chairs: Wesley Hall Inc. #888, custom finish; table: Sarreid, Ltd. Stylist, Lynn McBride; photography, Cheryl Dalton.

Pages 22–25: Architect, A. J. (Tony) Tamborello, AIA, 3621 Yupon St., Houston, TX 77006; 713/522-9496. Interior Design, Martha Brooks, 3831 Glenheather, Houston, TX; 281/444-5216. Living room paint, Benjamin Moore 1679 eggshell finish. Note: Benjamin Moore has revised its palette and paint system; contact your local Benjamin Moore dealer for an updat-

ed version of this color. Visit the website at www.benjaminmoore.com to find the dealer nearest you. Trim throughout, Benjamin Moore Linen White; entry and kitchen, custom-mixed red. Fabrics: Martha Washington chair, Robert Allen Orcott/Brick (back, Balzac/Lacquer) with Heartwell/Red cording. Henredon sofas covered in Scalamandre fabric; Bushy Brush fringe/Natural, Robert Allen (to the trade). Page 24: Kitchen tiles: Ceramic Tile International Antiqua #101 Red and Antiqua #115 Almond, 4x4 tiles. Stylist, Joetta Moulden; photography, Cheryl Dalton.

Pages 26–27: Dining room paint: ICI Ming Ivory #847 60YY 77/180. Den paint: ICI Crescent Inn #763 45YY 70/193. Stylist, Wade Scherrer; photography, Peter Krumhardt.

HOW CAN I CHANGE THE SENSE OF SPACE?

Page 31: Interior design, Rhea Crenshaw, Rhea Crenshaw Interiors, Memphis, TN. Stylist, Julie Azar; photography, Emily Minton.

Page 32: Interior design, Sheila Barron, Barron & Stoll Interior Design, 2402 Lincoln St., Evanston, IL 60201; 847/864-4778. Sleigh bed: Carson Pirie Scott, Milwaukee, WI; 800/374-3000. Bed quilt, local quilt gallery. Bed sheets: The Ralph Lauren Home Collection, New York, NY; 212/642-8700. Linens, throw, chaise quilt, table: antiques. Fabric for draperies and shams: Waverly, 800/423-5881; www.waverly.com. Pink lamp, Pursuit of Happiness, 1524 Chicago Ave., Evanston, IL 60201; 847/869-2040. Cornices: Hebron Antique Gallery; 815/648-4794. Paint: custom mix. Painting over headboard: Donald Stuart Antiques, 571 Lincoln Ave., Winnetka, IL 60093; 847/501-4454. Wall color similar to Sherwin Williams Parisienne SW 1600. Photography, Jon Jensen; field editors Sally Mauer, Hilary Rose.

Page 33: Interior design, Kelly G. Amen, P.O. Box 66447, Houston, TX 77266; www.kga.net. Walls: Benjamin Moore 5/E 1414 eggshell finish. See Note under Pages 22–25. Bed covering, antique bark painting. Chair, by John Palmer, Houston; www.johnpalmerart.com. Ottoman, compound sculpture from Kelly Gale Amen Design. Stylist, Joetta Moulden; photography, Cheryl Dalton.

Page 35: Living room paint: Behr Brand, Shadow Olive 2B6-2. Stylist, Wade Scherrer; photography, Peter Krumhardt.

Page 36: Wall color: custom-mix, similar to Sherwin Williams Primitive Green SW 1421; beaded-board wainscot and trim: similar to Waverly Pearly White WP 157. Sink, Parisian, St. Thomas Creations, 619/336-3980. Toothbrush holder, shower caddy, soap dish, wall sconces, accordian mirror: Pottery Barn, 800/922-5507. Photography, King Au, Studio Au.

Page 37: Wall and floor tile #315024 Stone Classics Slate, 12-inch squares, mottled purple, from Daltile; 800/933-8453. Wood blinds, Country Woods, #837 dark walnut, Hunter Douglas Window Fashions; 800/227-8953. Dresser with drop-in sink, #197-607 Bombe Chest, aged pine, Cambridge Cherry Collection, Drexel Heritage Furnishings. Black and silver mirror, #SF-53 Shield, Jo-Liza International. Wallpaper, Waverly #572952 Castille Vine, Jewel. Photography, Greg Sheideman.

Pages 38–39: Interior design, Gregor D. Cann, Canndesign@aol.com; Boston, 617/293-6078; Palm Springs, CA, 760/318-7925. Yellow walls, Martin Senour Safflower; blue walls, Benjamin Moore Pool Party. Floors: loading-dock paint. Photography: Eric Roth.

Pages 40–41: Color help: Lou Ann Bauer, ASID, 415/621-7262. Ceiling paint: Benjamin Moore 305; periwinkle wall paint, Benjamin Moore 1423. See Note under Pages 22–25. Chairs, sofa, Flexform through Limn Co., San Francisco, 415/543-5466; carpet, by Bauer Interior Design; window shade fabric, Henry Cassen, HC90195, Decorators Walk, Plainview, NY (to the trade). Page 41: Yellow walls, Benjamin Moore 305; small painted cupboard, David Marsh Furniture through Zia, 1310 10th St., Berkeley, CA 94710; 510/528-2377. Dining chairs: Palacek (to the trade). Painting of diver by Joyce Robertson. Photography, Jon Jenson; field editor Carla Howard.

Pages 42–45: Interior design, Kelly G. Amen, see under Page 33. Wall colors, Benjamin Moore: lavender, 3/E 1454; café au lait, 4/E 1106; moss green, 4/D 1532; terra-cotta, 4/D 1195. Base for trim, 1/C 989. See Note under Pages 22–25. Coffee table, triangle pillows on sofa, KGA Design, www.kga.net. Stylist, Joetta Moulden; photography, Cheryl Dalton.

WHAT COLOR SHOULD I PAINT MY CEILING?

Pages 49–50: Interior design, Roberta Ketchin, see under Pages 17–21. Wallcovering: Westgate Fabrics (www.westgatefabrics.com), Inc., Canton WP-8214 Cobalt 27-0. Coverlet fabric, Payne Fabrics, Inc., pattern XP3059, color 270. Dust skirt fabric: Westgate Fabrics, pattern 1-2911, color 28-0. Drapery fabrics: panel, Duralee Fabrics, Ltd. (to the trade), pattern T30493, color Snow; band, Robert Allen, Caswell/Tomato. Table skirt fabrics: skirt, P. Collins, Ltd. (to the trade), #3661-A/Cornflower; band, Robert Allen, Caswell/Tomato. Chair, ottoman fabric: Wesley Hall, Inc., discontinued. Bench fabric: Harden, discontinued. Page 50: Wallcovering, F. Schumacher & Co., pattern Cage à Oiseaux/Coral, 523332. Bench fabric, F. Schumacher & Co., discontinued. Stylist, Lynn McBride; photograhy, Cheryl Dalton.

Page 51: Pillows on sofa: Décor de l'ile, Charleston, SC; 843/723-6022. Field editor, Lynn McBride; photography, Rick Taylor.

Pages 52–55: Interior designer, Kelly G. Amen, see under Page 33. Decorative paint finishes and glazes: Theo Ostler, 713/524-7611. Base paints: Benjamin Moore. Pearlized glaze, iridescent white latex paint, from artist's supply shop, thinned and brushed over latex base coat (eggshell finish). Stylist, Joetta Moulden; photography, Cheryl Dalton.

Pages 56–57: Left: Wall color similar to Sherwin Williams Buttercream SW 1659. Ceiling color similar to Sherwin Williams Farm Fresh SW 1422. Stylist, Lynn McBride; photography, Cheryl Dalton. Center: Skip Sroka and Cynthia Polson, Sroka Design, Inc., Washington, DC. Wall finish: The Valley Craftsmen Ltd., 3535 Clipper Mill Rd., Baltimore, MD 21211; 410/366-7077. Window fabric: Brunschwig & Fils, 212/838-7878 (to the trade). Photography, Ross Chapple; field editor, Eileen Deymier. Right: Interior design, Roberta Ketchin, see under Pages 17–21. Ceiling color similar to Sherwin Williams Lavender Blue SW 1248. Table beside stairs, 18th-century English. Fabric on bench: discontinued. Ottoman: Baker Furniture, 800/592-2537. Fabric on ottoman: Greeff: Farmer's Friend 3064017, color Grass. (Greeff is an F. Schumacher company, to the trade; for more information, visit www.fschumacher.com). All other chairs: French antiques. Fabric on chair in right foreground and back cushion on chair in front of window: Hot Lime from Satin Chintz collection, Schumacher (to the trade).

Red check fabric: Red-and-Yellow, Designers Guild (to the trade). Window treatment fabric: Misticanza Salsa #F570/02, Osborne & Little (to the trade). Field editor, Lynn McBride; photography, Ross Chapple.

Page 58: Interior design, Kelly Bryant O'Neal, Legacy Trading Co., 3699 McKinney Ave., #104, Dallas, TX 75204; 214/953-2222. Paint colors: soffit and ceiling, Benjamin Moore Shaker Beige softened with light whitewash (flat latex paint, dry powdery coat); bottom, Benjamin Moore Burnt Sienna colorwashed with Iron Black; trim, Benjamin Moore Iron Black. Photography, Jenifer Jordan; field editor Diane Carroll.

Page 59: Architect, Marc Tarasuck, AIA, and Associates, 744 G St., Studio 206, San Diego, CA 92101; 619/262-0100. Paintings: Fiestaware series—Judith Jarcho, artist, through J. Jarcho Studios, San Diego, 888/518-2424; www.jjarcho.com. Paint: Benjamin Moore; ceiling, HC 133; walls, 313, cabinets, OC 17. See Note under Pages 22–25. Toaster, mixer, diner stools, dish rack: William Sonoma, 800/541-2233. Vintage pottery: architect's personal collection. Light fixtures, ceiling fan, light: Lamps Plus, 800/360-5267. Photography, Ed Gohlich; field editor, Andrea Caughey.

Page 60: Interior designer, Kelly Bryant O'Neal, see under Page 58. Paint: Benjamin Moore Redd Yellow. Photography, Jenifer Jordan; field editor Diane Carroll.

Page 61: Paint, decorative finishes, Joan Drown Paints, 7112 SE 14th Ave., Portland, OR 97202. Most antiques: Stars, 7027 SE Milwaukee, Portland, OR 97202; 503/239-0346; also Stars Northwest, 503/220-8180; Stars and Splendid, 503/235-5990; More Stars, 503/235-9142. Leopard pillows, Celia Mason, 1577 Chemetka NE, Salem, OR 97301; 503/362-3245. Pillars: Bernadette Breu Antiques, 1134 NW Everett, Portland, OR 97209; 503/226-6565. Photography, Philip Clayton Thompson.

Page 62: Wall color similar to Sherwin Williams Hopi Squash SW 1656. Photography, Philip Thompson; regional editor, Donna Pizzi.

Page 63: Interior design, Kenneth Melton. Wall color similar to Sherwin Williams Apricot Lily SW 1617. Moonbeam chairs 0531-044 (1784-02); sofa, P490-348 (1720-90) Thomasville Furniture Inds., Inc.; for a dealer near you, call 800/225-0265. Area rug, 106 Hopscotch, 150/gold—Capel, Inc. 831 North Main St., Troy, NC 27371; 800/334-3711. Gas fireplace, Majestic Co., 800/525-1898. Window coverings: "Silhouette Shades," Hunter Douglas Window Fashions; 800/227-8953. Photography, Geoffrey Gross.

Page 64: Interior designer, Dana Donaldson, ASID; fax 203/438-7008. Photography, Tom McWilliam; field editor, D.J. Carey.

Page 65: Paint: below chair rail: Behr Brand, Ginger Root 2A6-3, hand-striped with white. Above chair rail: Behr Brand, Washed Silk 2B6-1. Color help and stylist, Wade Scherrer; photography, Peter Krumhardt.

Page 66: Inset photo: Walls: Benjamin Moore Forest Green, 800/826-2623. Trim, Benjamin Moore Panacia White. Stylist, Joe Boehm; photography, William Stites. Right: Ceiling color similar to Sherwin Williams Madcap Violet SW1246. Lower walls, color similar to Sherwin Williams Buttercream SW 1659.

Page 67: Designer, Sandra Holtzinger, 3491 Airport Rd., Cle Elum, WA 98922. Photography, Michael Jensen; regional contributor, Trish Maharam.

SHOULD THE TRIM ALWAYS BE WHITE?

Page 71: Interior design, Ballantine Interiors, Laura Miller, St. Louis, MO; 314/361-0034. Ralph Lauren Hunting Coat Red; Laura says the secret to success with this paint is to prime first, using a white primer to which you add as much black pigment as you can get into the can. All trim, Benjamin Moore HC 174. See Note under Pages 22–25. Ceilings, Benjamin Moore ceiling white. Stylist, Mary Anne Thomson; photography, Cheryl Dalton.

Page 72: Interior designer: Sally Dixon, Sally Dixon Interiors, 3639 Charles St., San Diego, CA 92106; 619/225-1668. Walls: terra-cotta color applied with a ragged treatment. Paint: Dunn-Edwards Paint Corp., 4885 E. 52nd Place, Los Angeles, CA 90040; call 800/537-4098 for a local retail source. Photography, Ed Gohlich; field editor, Andrea Caughey.

Page 73: Walls: Martha Stewart Seaweed, trim Benjamin Moore HC 174.

Page 74: Wall color: Valspar American Traditions/Georgian Amber Gold; painted trim, Valspar Bright White (flat finish). Stylist, Wade Scherrer; photography, Peter Krumhardt.

Page 75: Top: paint, decorative finishes, Joan Drown Paints, see under Page 61. Most antiques: see under Page 61. Photography Philip Clayton Thompson. Bottom: See under Pages 7–15.

Page 76: Architect, Kramer Architects, 7960 Unit D, Old Georgetown Rd., Bethesda, MD 20814; 301/652-5700. Kitchen design: Don Singman, Kitchen Techniq, Inc., Rockville, MD 20852; 301/231-0633. Chairs at island, Lucky Acorn Chairs by artist Thomas Lynch, P.O. Box 114, Rock Cave, WV 26234; 304/924-5852. Photography, D. Randolph Foulds; field editor Heather Lobdell.

Page 77: Walls: Benjamin Moore Soft Fern with gold-leafed molding at ceiling. Interior designer, Kelly Bryant O'Neal, see under Page 58. Photography, Jenifer Jordan; field editor, Diane Carroll.

Page 79: Interior design, Kelly G. Amen, see under Page 33. Walls: Benjamin Moore 5/E 1414 eggshell finish; see Note under Pages 22–25. Stylist, Joetta Moulden; photography, Cheryl Dalton.

Page 80: For wall color, see under Page 74. Original woodwork (window frames, mantel, cabinet door frames flanking fireplace) was stripped and polyurethaned. New wood (cased opening, cabinet doors) was stained with oil-base walnut stain, sanded down, then stained with a custom-mix of red and brown oil-base stains to match original wood. Stylist, Wade Scherrer; photography, Peter Krumhardt.

Page 81: Paint: Luminaria by Martha Stewart Everyday Paint, Kmart; 800/635-6278. Mirror, buffet, cement urns, light fixture: antiques. Light fixture shades: Pottery Barn: 800/922-5507. Photography, Bob Greenspan Photography; field editor, Susan Andrews.

Pages 82–83: Wall color similar to Sherwin Williams Filtered Sun SW1646. Green leather-cushioned chair: L & J.G. Stickley, Manlius, NY; 315/682-5500. Coffee table, vase and bowl on table, pillow: Rejuvenation Lamp & Fixture Co., Portland, OR; 888/343-8548; www.rejuvenation.com. Photography, Jon Jensen; regional contributor, Barbara Mundall.

I CAN'T CHANGE MY CARPET. WHAT SHOULD I DO?

Pages 86–87: Walls: ICI Paint: Ming Ivory #847 60YY 77/180. Stylist, Wade Scherrer; photography, Peter Krumhardt.

Pages 88–91: Walls (after), Ralph Lauren Country/Jack Rabbit C001A. Fabrics, Waverly: duvet, Provincial Estates Inga/Oyster 664032; pillow shams, duvet trim, Provincial Estates Baltic Brocade/Oyster 664052; draperies, bedskirt, neckroll pillow, Provincial Estates Stockholm Stripe/Oyster 647260. For more information, call 800/423-5881 or visit the website, www.waverly.com. Drapery rod, Kirsch Products; 8-foot 3-inch wood pole, ball finials, bracket, rings; visit the website at www.kirsch.com to find a dealer near you. Stylist, Wade Scherrer; photography, Peter Krumhardt.

Pages 92–93: Walls, Benjamin Moore Neon Celery 2031-60; bedding, "Coming Up Daisies," The Land of Nod, P.O. Box 1404, Wheeling, IL 60090; call 800/933-9904 for a catalog. Stylist, Wade Scherrer; photography, Peter Krumhardt.

Pages 94–97: Fabric, Waverly; sofa slipcover Limerick/Khaki 647096; pillows White Russian Paisley/ Woodland 601607; 800/423-5881; www.waverly.com. Page 95: Carpet in room: "Elegant Manor" (Golden Olive), 9051-Mohawk Carpet; 800/882-8846; left to right, insets: T1898 "Royal Classic" (Chiffon Blue), 9848-Shaw Ind., Inc. 800/441-7429; 2545 "Portofino" (Desiree), 729-Mohawk Carpet; "Diamond Bar" (Spruce Bud 5708)-Shaw Ind., Inc. Page 96: Carpet in room, 9336 "Florence" (Paprika), 938-Masland Carpets, Inc., P.O. Box 11467, Mobile AL 36671; 800/633-0468. Inset photos, left to right: "Garden Flower" (Natural), 980/0-The Wilton Gallery; 800/882-8846. 56846, "Statsly Tartans" (Windsor Navy), 46445-Philadelphia; 800/882-8846. "Cavatina" (Imperial), 885-Masland Carpets, Inc. Photography, Hopkins Associates; design, Joseph Boehm.

Page 99: Styling, Wade Scherrer; photography, Peter Krumhardt. Bottom photos, design by Mark C. Holub, Des Moines, IA.

I LOVE MY SOFA. WHAT COLOR DO I PAINT MY WALLS?

Pages 102–105: Floral sofa—Fabrics, Waverly: Sofa, Rosebank/Lapis 664552; wicker chair, Two by Two Party Plaid/Sky 647304; pillows, Vineyard Ticking/Buttercup 647686. Paint: Behr Paints, Traditional Home/Meadow Path TH 13, Craftsman Moss TH 69, Regatta TH 68. Striped sofa—Fabrics, Waverly: Sofa, Shawl Stripe/Rose 647780; draperies, Kensington Coral/Rose 647803; table skirt: Pimlico Plaid/Jute 647790. Paints: Behr Paints, Midwest Living/Spiced Cider MWL 16; Antique Plum MWL 19; Country Home/Beeswax, CH 36. All trim, Country Home/Plaster, CH 15. Stylist, Wade Scherrer; photography, Peter Krumhardt.

Pages 106–107: Drapery, bed skirt, and chair fabric: Pindler & Pindler, Inc., Moorpark, CA; 805/531-9090 (to the trade). Pillow shams: Horchow Home Catalog; 800/456-7000. Towels: Ralph Lauren Home Collection; 212/642-8700. Photography, Jon Miller, Hedrich-Blessing; field editors, Sally Mauer and Hilary Rose.

Pages 108–109: Interior design: Amy Cornell Hammond, Cornell & Co. Interior Design, Upper Marlboro, MD. Fabrics, Brunschwig & Fils, available through decorators. Wall finish, Bryon S. Owens, 4 Leslie Drive, Indian Head, MD 20640; 301/743-7677. Upholstered pieces, headboard, hangings, bed skirt, lamp with pierced shade, handpainted pillow, all accessories: Cornell & Co. Interior Design. Photography, Ross Chapple; field editor, Eileen Deymier. Location: Southern Maryland Decorators' Showhouse, Newburg, MD.

Pages 110–111: Stylist, Lynn McBride; photography, Cheryl Dalton.

Pages 112–113: Interior design, Ballantine Interiors, see Page 71. Walls: Benjamin Moore 200; trim, Benjamin Moore HC 174. See Note under Pages 22–25. Stylist, Mary Ann Thomson; photography, Cheryl Dalton.

Pages 114–115: GE Reveal bulbs from GE Lighting are incandescent but give off a crisp light that appears truer than the light of ordinary incandescent bulbs. A natural earth element added to the glass gives the unlit bulb a pale blue color; the earth element filters out the yellow cast. Bulbs are available in a variety of types and a range of wattages; look for them at home centers, mass merchandisers, hardware stores, and supermarkets.

WHAT COLOR WILL LOOK BEST WITH MY WOOD FURNITURE?

Page 117: Interior design, Sandra Holtzinger, 3491 Airport Rd., Cle Elum, WA 98922. Photography, Michael Jensen; regional contributor, Trish Maharam.

Pages 118–119: Interior design, Ballantine Interiors; see under Page 71. Wall color: Porter Paint White Opal. Drapery fabric, P. Kauffman, Lydia Irwin design; available through Calico Corners, www.calicocorners.com. Styling, Mary Anne Thomson; photography, Cheryl Dalton.

Page 120: Wall paint: Martin Senour Paints, Williamsburg Colors: above chair rail, #1018 Apothecary Shop Blue Light, below chair rail, #1017 Apothecary Shop Blue Medium. Call 800/677-5270 for store information. Throw, pelmet fabric, #50744 Merlot, Pompeii, and Willow from Schumacher; 800/332-3384 (to the trade). Produced by Edward Kemper Design; photography, King Au/Studio Au.

Page 121: Left: See under Pages 17–21. Right: See under Page 71. Wall color Benjamin Moore 200; see Note under Pages 22–25.

Page 122: Left: Paint, Ralph Lauren Safari/Reed SA 18C. Center: Paint, Martin Senour Paints, Williamsburg Colors, #1032 Market Square Green Medium. Right: See under Page 71.

Page 123: Paint, Benjamin Moore Bennington Gray. Design, credits, see under Pages 7–15.

Pages 124–125: Paints: A: Valspar Paints, American Traditions/Hunter Green 789-3; B: Valspar, Romantic Revival/English Ivy 793-3; C: Behr, Vermouth 3B1-1; D: Waverly Paints, Utah Sky WD-258; E: Waverly Paints, Tangerine WD-183; F: Valspar, Color Spectrum/Casba Melon 264B-4. Styling, Wade Scherrer; photography, Peter Krumhardt.

HOW CAN I UPDATE MY KITCHEN AND BATH?

Pages 127–130: Interior design, Ballantine Interiors; see under Page 71. Cabinet and tile paint, Benjamin Moore HC 174; see Note under Pages 22–25. Soffit and stairwell walls, Ralph Lauren Cottswald Breeches.

Page 131: Paint, Sherwin Williams 1430; call 800/474-3794 for store information. Curtain fabric, Waverly, Old Fashion Favorite/Daphne 304640; call 800/423-5881 or visit the website at www.waverly.com. Stencils from Designer Stencils, 2503 Silverside Road, Wilmington, DE 19810. Stylist, Catherine Kramer; photography, William Hopkins.

Pages 132–133: Design, see under Page 71. Wallpaper above tile, Stroheim & Rohm.

Pages 134–135: Page 134, right: Wallpaper, Seabrook DG269; call 800/238-9152 for the dealer nearest you. Page 135: Wall paint, Behr Brand Sterling Cloud 3B40-1; cabinets, Behr Brand Foam Flower 3B31-1. Styling, Wade Scherrer; photography, Peter Krumhardt.

Pages 136–137: Kitchen walls: ICI Paints, Wood Lily #736 40YY 83/129. Dining room walls: see under Pages 26–27.

HOW DO I WORK WITH THE COLOR OF MY BRICK?

Page 139: Styling, Lynn McBride; photography, Cheryl Dalton.

Pages 140–141: Inset and Page 141: Architect, John K. Wolff, Wolff + Lyon Architects. Photography, Tim Murphy/Foto Imagery; field editor, Mindy Pantiel. Page 140: Interior design, Jean J. Comb-Meade, ASID, and Sara Scott Cullen, Birmingham, MI. Photography, Beth Singer; field editor, Suzy Farbman.

Pages 142–143: Paint, Page 142: Custom-mixed color with glazes. Page 143: Walls, beams, Ralph Lauren Safari/Reed SA 18C; ceiling, Ralph Lauren Papyrus SA17C. Stylist, Wade Scherrer; photography, Peter Krumhardt.

Page 145: Paint: Mautz Paint Co., Pigeon Isle, Sassy Mauve; P.O. Box 7068, Madison, WI 53707; 608/255-1661. Chair and ottoman fabric, Calico Corners, VA. For store locations, write Walnut Road Business Park, 203 Gale Lane, Kennett Square, PA 19348; or call 800/213-6366. Boomerang tabletop, French Sycamore #1143-Formica Corp., 10155 Reading Road, Cincinnati, OH 45241; 800/367-6422. Screen: Custom-made by Nekoda Decorative Folding Screens, 888/516-6247. Screen stain: Wild Berry from Sherwin-Williams, 31500 Solon Road, Solon, OH 44139; 800/457-9566. Screen fabric, Calico Corners, Caldwel; for store information, see above. Floor lamps, throw, Spiegel, 800/774-3435; www.spiegel.com. Photography, Hopkins Associates; produced by Heidi Kluzak.

I LIKE WHITE, BUT HOW CAN I MAKE IT INTERESTING?

Pages 149–150: Interior design, Connie Driscoll. Photography, Sam Gray; regional contributor, Estelle Bond Guralnick.

Page 151: Photography, Jamie Hadley; design, Laurel Louderbach.

Pages 152–157: Styling, Mary Anne Thomson; photography, Alise O'Brien.

Pages 158–59: Interior design, John Wiltgen, John Robert Wiltgen Design, Inc., 70 W. Hubbard St., Suite 205, Chicago, IL 60610; 312/744-1151. Sofa: Urbana, 2900 Mead Ave., Santa Clara, CA 95051; 408/988-3464. Table: AXI, 131 N. Gilbert St.., Fullerton, CA 92833; 714/526-8184. Floor lamps: George Kovacs Lighting, Inc., 6725 Otto Road, Glendale, NY 11385; 718/628-5201. Chenille throw: Textillery Weavers; 800/223-7673. Photography, James Yochum; field editor, Elaine Markoutsas.

Pages 160–161: Interior design, Julia Doyle, J. Doyle Design, 36 E. 20th St., 8th Floor, New York, NY 10003; 212/533-5455. Settee with pink cushion: Settee, design by Eliel Saarinen, available through Arkitektura, 212/334-5570. Settee cushion, gold ottoman, white sofa, pillows: J. Doyle Design. Ottoman fabric, Abruzzi 7006-9, Bergamo Fabrics, Inc.; 212/888-3333 (to the trade; contact an interior designer or home furnishings store). Tricolor Swedish side chair: antique. Whitewashed oak end tables: Billy Baldwin–Ventry, through Hinson & Co., 718/482-1100 (to the trade). Table lamps: Jerrystyle, 760/416-9300 (manufacturer; call for the name of a local store). Photography, Tom McWilliam; field editor, Patricia O'Shaughnessy.

INDEX